CW00429199

DON'T LET
THEM BAG
THE NINES

DON'T LET THEM BAG THE NINES

THE FIRST WORLD WAR MEMOIR
OF A DE HAVILLAND PILOT –
CAPTAIN F. WILLIAMS MC DFC

FOREWORD BY PATRICK BISHOP

Captain Williams joined the RFC as test pilot, later flying DH4s in photo-reconnaissance and bomber raids over Germany, and winning the DFC and Croix de Guerre.

James Coyle's wife inherited his memoirs from her mother, Williams' sister. He decided that Captain Williams' manuscript would be of interest to a wider audience, and with the help of his daughter, Alana, put it forward for publication.

First published 2019

The History Press
97 St George's Place, Cheltenham,
Gloucestershire, GL50 3QB
www.thehistorypress.co.uk

© Captain Williams and James Coyle, 2019

The right of Captain Williams and James Coyle
to be identified as the Authors of this work
has been asserted in accordance with the
Copyright, Designs and Patents Act 1988.

All rights reserved. No part of this book may be reprinted
or reproduced or utilised in any form or by any electronic,
mechanical or other means, now known or hereafter invented,
including photocopying and recording, or in any information
storage or retrieval system, without the permission in writing
from the Publishers.

British Library Cataloguing in Publication Data.
A catalogue record for this book is available from the British Library.

ISBN 978 0 7509 9131 5

Typesetting and origination by The History Press
Printed and bound in Great Britain by TJ International Ltd

CONTENTS

FOREWORD BY PATRICK BISHOP

The air war over the trenches produced some excellent books. Air fighting was new and the novelty of it all propelled many on both sides of the conflict into print. Some of the writing, like *Sagittarius Rising* by Cecil Lewis, was sublime. Other efforts, like James McCudden's *Flying Fury* and Manfred von Richtofen's *The Red Fighter Pilot*, were unadorned but strikingly authentic. All conveyed to an eager audience the raw drama of what it was like to fly, kill and die in the heroic age of military aviation.

Almost all the output, however, was seen from the perspective of those flying 'scouts' or fighters. For the first part of the war these one- or two-man machines did most of the work: spotting for the guns, photographing the enemy lines and trying to shoot down enemy aircraft doing the same. In the latter part of the war, the bombing of German communications lines and war factories became an increasingly important part of the activities of the RFC and (from 1 April 1918) RAF. It is this part of the air war that Frederick Williams' memoir deals with. Though it was not apparent at the time, bombing would come to be the *raison d'etre* of the British Air Force, and Williams' testimony is all the more valuable for bearing witness to the birth of the process.

'Willie', as his comrades knew him, was clearly a man of his time, and the tone is restrained and understated. His emotional reticence, however, only increases the impact when feelings show through. At one level the book provides a fascinating account of the life of a bombing squadron in the first half of 1918 just as things were hotting up. The pilots, observers and ground staff lived in primitive conditions in the dank heart of rural eastern France, struggling as much with the weather as the enemy. When they did get airborne the experience was a mixture of long stretches of boredom interspersed with sharp passages of terror.

'For the ordinary flying officers, these raids were simply unpleasant experiences,' he wrote. 'There was nothing for the pilots to do but keep in formation for several hours under shellfire, the actual dropping of the bombs being our only recreation; for the observer there was nothing but the constant watch for enemy machines. For both, in fact, there was little else to do but wonder if they would get home again.'

Williams is frank about the fear he frequently felt and the human cost of the 'offensive spirit' inculcated in squadrons by their commander in chief, Hugh Trenchard. In the circumstances, there was little choice but numb acceptance. He remembered that one day:

... after breakfasting at 9:30, we strolled up to the hangars, where mechanics were at work cleaning and overhauling our faithful mounts; my rigger was busily removing the mud, which had been thrown up by my tyres onto the under surface of my lower planes, while my fitter inspected one of my four magnetos.

Presently I came across the Technical Sergeant Major, and we talked about old days at Lilbourne.

'It was a pity you ever left the Squadron, Sir,' he remarked, 'we were talking in the Mess the other night, and we said you would have had a flight by now if you had come out with us.'

'Oh well, you can't tell, I might have been killed by now Sergeant Major.'

'Oh no, Sir, you haven't been killed, so you wouldn't have been killed.' This fatalism struck me as being eminently suitable for an airman, and I tried to adopt much the same attitude.

Williams was an early example of the ethos that the RAF sought to cultivate. He was skilful but modest, brave without advertising his courage and exhibited that slight detachment from the business of war that marked many airmen. It is wonderful that his memoir is now seeing the light of day.

INTRODUCTION BY JAMES COYLE

This book is the product of a manuscript found in an RAF trunk from the First World War. Originally entitled 'With the Rolls Fours', it belonged to my wife's uncle, Captain Frederick Williams MC DFC.

I first became aware of 'Uncle's Trunk' in 1967 when his sister, Jane, stayed with my wife, Janet, and myself. The trunk followed us around to various houses; sometimes the contents would be looked at but not often. It contained various items of interest from Captain Williams' time in the RFC/RAF, including medals, log books and even bits of his plane. The majority of these are now held by the RAF Museum in Hendon.

Williams was born in Australia to English parents in 1898. The family had a property in the semi-arid area of Queensland, which they were eventually forced to abandon due to a prolonged period of drought, the lack of water and grass making it impossible to feed the stock. They moved to Switzerland, where he and Jane were educated. There he learnt French and German, which was to prove useful in his work in Germany after the war.

Williams joined the RFC in April 1916 and was sent to France in March the following year. He was initially posted to 66 Squadron and later joined 55 Squadron, serving with them until the end of the war. He was described by the RAF as 'an excellent leader and most able instructor', and recognised 'for [his] conspicuous gallantry and devotion to duty during operations. He took part in a number of long-distance raids and photographic reconnaissances, showing great gallantry and skill under difficult conditions. He destroyed three enemy aircraft and drove down two out of control. Throughout he showed great keenness and determination.'

In a letter to his mother, Williams described a mission when his formation encountered twenty enemy planes, declaring, 'I do not intend to let the boys down I am supposed to guard and if things get too hot may God give me the courage to drive them off or go down fighting for I have never turned my back upon the Hun or devil yet!'

Despite his determination to protect his colleagues, he did not lack respect for his opponents, and in the same letter he observed:

> One thing I will say for the enemy they have some jolly stout fellows amongst them, and when it comes to burying our dead they always do it nicely and put over the graves 'Brave English Soldiers who died for their Fatherland in the fighting by Ypres July 1915', for example, and what more glorious thing could be written over one's grave than '*Tapfer Englischer FLièger im Lufer Kampf gefallen*'.

Following the Armistice, Williams was posted to Germany where he was able to put to use his skills in German and French. He was subsequently posted to Mesopotamia with the RAF, where his service was brought to an abrupt halt when he contracted polio. He was sent to a hospital in Egypt and then brought back to England by ship. He settled in Devon and became involved in the development of St Loyes Hospital. He eventually became the superintendent, despite his disability, and was awarded the MBE in 1950. Captain Williams died in 1963 in Devon.

I decided that Captain Williams' manuscript may be of interest to a wider audience, and with the help of my daughter, Alana, put it forward for publication. I hope you will enjoy this insight into the First World War experiences of one of Britain's early pilots.

James Coyle, 2019

Uncle's Trunk: Captain Williams' trunk containing various items of interest from his time in the RFC/RAF.

1

A PRODIGAL'S RETURN

A message had just come through to say that the weather was fit for flying at Marquise, and the floating-jacketed ferry-pilots were hurrying over from Lympne, hoping to catch the boat back at once, and spend the evening in town.

I had been fortunate enough to spend Christmas 1917 on leave, and was now returning to France. Machine after machine left the ground; at last I secured the services of a mechanic to start my engine, and set off in my SE5.

The clouds were very low, it was dark and misty; I did not like the idea of crossing the Channel at 300 feet, so climbed up into the mist. For the next five minutes I was enveloped in the thick, wet blanket of cloud, but I was not uneasy; we had never heard of ice forming in these conditions. At 5,000 feet I caught a glimpse of very blue sky, and came out above the snowy tablel and, a few seconds later, into brilliant sunshine.

From 10,000 feet, I could see the edge of the clouds in front of me, but they extended as far as the eye could see in every other direction. One thing puzzled me as I approached the edge of the clouds: I could see nothing but whiteness below and beyond. Was the coast of France shrouded in fog? This was hardly likely in so strong a wind. It was not until some minutes later that I realised that the peculiar whiteness was snow on the ground. My compass had served me well, I was right over Marquise. It was bitterly cold, and I was glad to go down and land; the ferry-pilots had not yet arrived.

After lunch Major Ainsley gave me another SE5, which I flew down to No. 2 Aircraft Depot at Candás, where I was then stationed as a test pilot. Six months previously, I had been sent back from 66 Squadron for a rest, after a fall of 8,000 feet completely out of control, owing to the jamming of my flying boot between the rudder bar and the end of the floorboard, during a scrap.

While at Candás I had flown over twenty different types; yet, I had never completely regained confidence as a Scout pilot. At first I wanted to go on Bristol Fighters with Johnny Milne, but when my friend was killed, I asked Major Baldwin to apply for me to go to 55, for I wanted to rejoin the squadron in which I had learnt to fly.

On 7 January I took a Bristol Fighter to Serney, near St Omer; on landing I was told to return to 2 A.D. immediately, as I had been posted away. A fast trip in a Crossley tender over the snow-covered roads, through the starlit night, and I was back at Candás. As I entered the mess, everyone looked at me in silence …

'Willie, you're off to 55,' said Captain Dunn, our C.O., as though delivering sentence of death. However, they gave me a very cheerful send-off next morning.

It was necessary to make a journey of some 200 miles in order to join 55 Squadron, which had now been sent to Tantonville, near Nancy, for the purpose of carrying out bombing raids into Germany. As no machine was allotted to the 41st Wing, to which 55 belonged, I was obliged to go by train, a proceeding that took two days.

On arriving at Nancy, I found the country a pleasant change after the flat plains of the North; everywhere were hills and valleys, pine woods and rivers. I was soon on my way to the squadron in one of the tenders. I felt intensely curious to see my new aerodrome; I knew that it was in a concealed position; yet, even so, I was surprised to see an R.F.C. flag flying beside the road between two woods. When the tender drew up, however, I saw that there were hangars behind the trees on the left and huts amongst those on the right.

I was received in the squadron office by Captain Colquhoun, the recording officer. Having given my particulars, I was taken into the mess for lunch. As both the C.O. and Captain Gray were on leave, I found that I knew no one in the squadron except Captain Waller, who had been a test pilot at 1 A.D., and some of the N.C.S.S and men, who had been with the squadron since it came out from Lilbourne.

As I have already said, our huts were hidden in the wood; they were, however, thoroughly well built and comfortable. I was given a room in 'The Lion's Den', with an excellent fellow called Matthews. There was a certain amount of rivalry between our abode and 'The Stiffs' Hut', which was occupied by the C.O., the flight commanders and a select company of flying officers.

A few days later we heard that Major Baldwin was taking over the 41st. Wing, and that Gray had been given command of 55. This was good news, for Baldwin would still be able to see to the well-being of his old squadron, while our new C.O. was a man who understood the difficulties of the region in which we were to operate.

The next day, Gray came back from leave; we had learned to fly together at Lilbourne, and here he was a Major, while I was still a 'poor Loot'; yet never once, by word or action, did he ever make me feel uncomfortable on this account.

'Hullo Willie, I'm damn glad to see you back in 55!' he said, grasping my hand, 'you'll be posted to "C" Flight, Farrington's, and you can have my old bus, *No. 6*.' It had never been Gray's practice to let the grass grow under his feet; here was a man under whom I must succeed.

It should have been stated that the squadron was practically out of action owing to the severity of the winter. The ground was deep in snow, the trees and hangars were covered in hoar frost of great thickness, from days of fog; so that, when I reported to Captain Farrington next morning, there was no question of flying.

It was with a feeling almost akin to reverence that I climbed into the seat of Gray's old machine, the war-scarred veteran of many a raid and reconnaissance, 'What a responsibility to take her over now!' I thought; little did I dream what lay before us both.

That night Baldwin came to say goodbye to the squadron; he caught sight of me as soon as he entered the mess, and shook hands, making me ridiculously happy for the rest of the evening. To quote from a letter:

After dinner there was a sort of dance; Puckridge was doing a tango with great skill, when he was tripped up, and sat down suddenly; his partner fell in the fire; but fortunately did not catch alight. After a very jolly evening, 'Ye Onchant Observers' Society' held a meeting in the bar, from which all 'chauffeurs' were excluded. The pilots attacked, led by the gallant Colonel himself. Not being able to burst open the door, we turned out their lights, and squirted them with fire extinguishers through the windows. The bar sounded like an inferno as all the perfectly good observers were getting soaked, and shouting and yelling inside.

The tin hat was put on their proceedings by someone throwing a stink bomb in amongst them; they were forced to surrender, and, as soon as the place had been aired, the attackers marched in. I had been sent for more ammunition, and arrived staggering under the weight of several large fire extinguishers after peace had been restored, much to everyone's amusement. Puckridge too, did not seem to realize that it was all over, for he presently tried to turn his pilot out again; but Collet took a soda water syphon and fired the contents down his neck!

The weather report for the next day being favourable, the celebrations ended at a reasonably early hour.

Next morning everyone was called long before it was light, and our hut soon resounded with shouting and singing. Matthews was dressing, so I got up too, in order to see the raids start for Karlsruhe, some 80 miles behind the Lines.

Next door there was the sound of boots being thrown about, Palmer was endeavouring to wake his pilot.

'Get up Oscar!' No reply.

'Get up Oscar, you'll be late for the show.' Another boot landed heavily.

'Umph?'

'Oscar, get up; I'm sure you'll be shot down today, probably in flames, or small pieces.'

'Umph?' Oscar did not appear to be very communicative at that hour in the morning.

I was astonished at the cheeriness with which the pilots and observers were setting out on what appeared to me to be a most hazardous adventure.

The departure of the raids was attended with great difficulty and danger, owing to the condition of the aerodrome. This was L shaped, only small strips of grass could be used for taking off and landing, unless the frost was hard enough to make the mud, which formed the remainder, safe for the heavy machines. On this occasion the de Havillands sank almost axle deep into the mud and snow as they ploughed their way across to the grass strip, their engines roaring, mechanics pushing, pulling and even trying to lift their wings.

At last they were all in position, but many of the pilots were very inexperienced and had not flown for several weeks; the start was an alarming spectacle.

Directly they had gone, I went up in *No. 6.* Just to the east of the aerodrome was a very striking landmark, a walled monastery perched on the top of a precipitous hill, which was known to us as Mount Zion, and to the French, I believe, as 'Le Colline Sacrée'.

I flew to Nancy, which was remarkably undamaged, considering its proximity to the Line, then down the somewhat indistinct trenches past Lunéville and so to the Vosges Mountains. I could see practically no activity on the ground on either side, while only one other machine was in the air; I took this to be French, as it was well on our side and was not being Archied.

The air was full of a soft haze, but the wide view from 11,000 feet was full of fascination; there to the north and east lay Germany, mysterious and brooding behind the mists; there too, beyond the dark mass of the wooded Vosges, must lie the Rhine … Presently I turned homewards, and managed to land on the little grass strip. The C.O. and others, who had been watching me arrive, ran out to help me in across the mud.

We now heard the distant rumble of twelve Rolls engines as our people passed over at a great height on their way to the Lines. It was difficult to make them out in the watery haze, which the sun had drawn from the damp ground; yet, the sight was very impressive. Two hours later all our machines were back; one or two pilots 'piled up' on landing, but fortunately no one was hurt. Karlsruhe had been bombed, and the junior members of the squadron were full of their experiences.

'My God, I thought Emma Gee had caught it! I couldn't see his bus for smoke.'

'Yes, I heard a terrific wonk right under my nose; I was shot clean out of my seat.'

'I heard a door slam just behind us; for a moment I thought we had lost our tail.'

'Did you see those Huns down low? Carroll was firing at one with a white fuselage.'

'Yes, but they never got near our height, they were waiting for a machine to fall out with engine trouble.'

Collet and Puckridge had an uncomfortable return journey; their engine had given signs of distress when they were still some 70 miles from the Line, and had been running irregularly all the way back.

Winter now closed down on us again. On several days it was possible to fly, and Farrington carried out several photographic reconnaissances, but long raids were out of the question. The days were still so short that it was necessary to start by noon, if night landings were not to be attempted on the return, but the fog usually persisted well into the afternoon. If it lifted at all, then it was found impossible to get the bomb-laden machines out unless the ground was frozen, as the mud was getting deeper and deeper; so that if the sun did break through during the morning, it often made the aerodrome unfit for use before the raids could start.

Meanwhile I was becoming thoroughly accustomed to my machine and the country for many miles round. I found *No. 6, B.3957*, was still an extremely fine machine; her speed and climb left nothing to be desired, while her controls were a joy to handle. She had originally been built for the R.N.A.S. and was equipped with two Vickers guns for the pilot and a little round turret, about 6 inches above the fuselage, for the observer's gun ring. I felt that she was no ordinary D.H. and there was a certain satisfaction in knowing that when the observer carried double Lewis guns, she was the most heavily armed machine on the Western Front!

It was great fun diving at the ground target at the end of the aerodrome. One day I had a sham fight with Waller; unfortunately, we were observed from the hangars, and when we got down, we were told that it was considered very bad form to stunt a D.H.4 and I believe some hard things were said about 'these bloody test-pilots' by junior members of the squadron, who could scarcely fly. One day, just after I landed, Collett asked me to have his younger brother, who was to join the squadron shortly, as my observer, and I was highly pleased at the implied compliment.

During this period many of us enjoyed long tramps through surrounding country. As the mess was sadly mismanaged by a person known as 'Lady Di', dinner at an estaminet in the neighbouring village of Xirocourt, where the food was as excellent as it was plentiful, became the fashion. I also spent several happy days with Gray looking for sites for new aerodromes in the squadron car, having previously found and photographed likely looking places from the air. These aerodromes would have been most useful if the war had lasted another year; as it was, at least one of them, Betancourt, was occupied before the Armistice.

We were always accompanied on these journeys by Roger, the squadron dog. Roger had been captured from the Germans by the French, and presented by them to 100 Squadron, when both they and 55 were at Ochey; however, he showed his good taste by attaching himself to 55, and travelled to Tantonville with the squadron.

One night, when some members of 100 Squadron had been dining with us, it was discovered that Roger was missing. We guessed at once what had become of him but were too late to prevent his captors driving off, although Waller fired his revolver at the tyres of their Crossley in his anxiety to stop them.

Next day a party went over to the Ochey to recover the dog; unfortunately they were detected and had to escape into the woods, with practically the whole of 100 Squadron after them, and an F.E. doing contact patrol close overhead. Their car was captured, but they managed to bag another and get home safely.

A few days later Miller, our equipment officer, was over at Ochey on business. It so happened that, during the course of his duties, he was standing on the aerodrome with Roger close at hand; at this moment a D.H.4 came in and landed, pulling up not 10 yards away. Miller seized up the Pom. and, before 100 Squadron realised what was happening, Roger was flying home again in Waller's machine.

We were so pleased that we immediately set off to Ochey in formation. Walmsley, our leader, took us across the aerodrome at 50 feet, and we bombarded the eight inhabitants with Verey lights, our fire being hotly returned. It was great fun, the danger of having one's machine set on fire or of burning down a perfectly good hangar containing valuable F.E.s hardly occurred to us.

Farrington managed to get his raids off the ground on 27 January. This was a very smart piece of work; they were all in the air within half an hour of being called! I was not given a place in this show, although I was now perfectly familiar with the country; it seemed to me that I was being kept back, but I thought it wisest to say nothing.

We had returned from taking photographs of desirable sites for aerodromes, and I was talking to A.M. Hodge, my observer, when we heard the distant drone of engines. Everyone began to search the northern sky, wondering if all our people would get back.

'There they are!' the flight sergeant was pointing; we made out four little dark objects flying together, then a fifth a little way behind, as it swept past a small fleecy cloud. After what seemed an age, another group appeared. As they landed we were amazed to see that many machines were still carrying their bombs. We learned afterwards that the second raid had lost touch with Farrington so badly that they had failed to notice when he dropped his bombs and had sailed over the objective without seeing it through the haze! Even so, it is difficult to understand why they did not get rid of their cargo on the way home.

That evening when Gray put up the orders in the mess, I found that I was to go to Kreuznach with the next show, but bad weather again set in. As it happened this was just as well for me, for on my next flight I noticed that my engine was not running perfectly. I mentioned this to Gray on landing, and he at once tested the machine himself. When he came down, he told me that the engine would have to be changed, as the reduction gear was damaged. Had I been on the way to Kreuznach, I might have been taken prisoner on my very first show.

2

OFFENBURG AND TRIER

The weather cleared before the new engine was ready, so that I was obliged to set out in old Diana 3 on my first show. As soon as we left the ground, I got into my position slightly above and behind Captain Fox on his right, while Van der Riet took up the corresponding position on his left.

We soon saw that the weather was hopeless over Germany. The Rhine Valley was entirely filled with low clouds, but the view of the snowy Alps, rising into the clear air, was magnificent.

Fox took us across the Lines at Badonviller at 12,000 feet. We were soon sailing over clouds; however, Fox went on for some time, hoping to find gaps. At last we were forced to turn back and land with our bombs, an annoying regulation preventing us from dropping them on the enemy in Alsace-Lorraine. Fortunately no one crashed.

A few days later, Roger vanished, and F.E.s flew excitedly over the aerodrome, so that we felt sure that 100 Squadron had done this thing. One evening six of us, led by Waller, set off in a tender for Ochey. About 2 miles from the aerodrome, the lights were put out and we drove on in darkness until we got to the foot of the hill, where we hid our car.

Waller went forward to ascertain the whereabouts of Roger, while we followed more slowly, guided by the F.E.s' landing lights. When we got to within 50 yards of the camp, we halted. An F.E. came booming overhead, invisible, except for the navigation lights, which looked like moving stars.

Suddenly shouting was heard from the camp, 'Turn out you! Those … have come from 55!'

Waller came rushing back, 'I know where he is, come on you chaps!'

We had just jumped up to follow him, when the darkness ahead was pierced with the flashes of a service revolver and several bullets passed between us; we immediately took shelter again.

Presently we heard voices; the C.O. of 100 Squadron himself was coming out to make peace. He regretted what had happened; it seemed that a certain N.C.O. had been somewhat the worse for drink. He then took us into the mess, where it was agreed that we should have Roger, on condition that we ceased to raid Ochey.

On returning to our tender we found that we had knocked a hole in the sump, through running into a small rock. We were obliged to go back and borrow a tender from our late foes, and finally got back to the squadron at 3 a.m.

Three hours later we were called; a singularly tactless orderly officer was standing at the door, emphasising the fact that it was a fine morning, with the most diabolical grin on his face.

Fox was again our leader, while Walmsley had the second raid. I now had *No. 6*, but, as A.M. Hodge was on leave, I took an officer named Bradly in my back seat.

Heavy banks of cloud made the success of the show doubtful from the first, but Fox took us across the Lines at Deutsches Avricourt. Away down below us, against a background of white, flew two quaint old French Caudrons; how friendly looked the snowy sea of vapour, now that it hid us from the anti-aircraft batteries on the Vosges!

Here and there we could see the tops of mountains or chalets in the forests below. Once or twice I caught the flash of a gun firing at us from the shadows below the clouds. A few shells burst amongst us, but Archy was not accurate. I now had my first glimpse of the Rhine, which could be seen in front of us, beyond the clouds, a straight silver line shining in the winter sunlight.

Presently we could see the dark mass of Strasbourg to the north. Soon we were crossing the Rhine with its rows of tiny barges; then we turned towards Offenburg, our objective. We had seen no enemy scouts, which I thought almost uncanny; perhaps they were waiting to come down on us 'out of the sun' as we dropped our bombs. I had an extra good look round; all our machines appeared to be in good formation; I could see no Huns above us. Below, everything appeared as though seen through clear water of great depth, owing to the haze. On our left lay the endless Black Forest, on our right the Rhine, and before us Offenburg.

Fox fired his white signal light, and soon afterwards his bombs fell off, going down quite slowly at first, it seemed, then gathering speed. The railway sidings and workshops were visible through my bomb-sight, though a trifle to the right for accuracy.

I wanted to turn to the right but could not do so without spoiling the formation, so I pulled my bomb release gear with a horrid feeling that I had missed my mark, but on looking round, I saw that Bradly was delighted with the result, and decided that he was quite a good observer after all.

As we turned homewards, we could see smoke rising from the objective, but many of the bombs had fallen in fields to the left.

We came in for more shelling on our way back to the Lines, and were glad to reach the protection of the clouds, over which we flew.

I saw the trenches at Saint-Dié through a gap in the clouds, but the French now took up the good work and shelled us with white shrapnel, which was fortunately most inaccurate. Fox now turned south, while Walmsley flew away northwest with the second raid. We flew over the clouds for a great distance; I was now getting very anxious, as we had been in the air for more than four hours and I did not know how much petrol I had left. It was obvious that Fox was lost, yet I felt it my duty to keep my place in the formation.

At last Fox took us down through the clouds, and we found ourselves over the fortress of Besançon. The formation had been broken up during the descent, so I felt free to turn northwards once more. I could see some of our machines flying round as though looking for a place to land, while others went away south. I signalled to Bradly to fire lights, but only one D.H. followed me.

It was uncomfortably dark and bumpy below the clouds, and the country beneath us was hopeless for a forced landing; so I flew on praying that I should find an aerodrome before my petrol gave out. I was south of my map, and had not the least idea how far it was from Besançon to Tantonville.

Presently I caught sight of an aerodrome near a little town nestling under the foothills of the Vosges. As I was gliding down with great thankfulness in my heart, a horrid thought flashed across my mind: had I unknowingly re-crossed the Lines? Was this a Hun aerodrome? But it was only for an instant, common sense told me that we were safe: there lay the Vosges away to the right, and the machines on the ground had French markings.

On landing, we were surrounded by excited Frenchmen of all ranks, who wanted to know if we had seen anything of the enemy machines that had passed over that morning. I do not think they quite believed us when we explained that it was at us their people had been firing.

Meanwhile Sansom landed, and we were all taken to the mess, where we were each given a glass of port and a couple of tiny sandwiches. Having just spent five hours in the air after a very hasty breakfast, we were extremely hungry yet did not like to ask for more.

Our hosts expressed much astonishment on hearing that we had been to Offenburg and warned us not to cross the Lines again, on account of powerful enemy chaser squadrons, who made this unwise.

Our machines had now been filled with petrol and oil, so we set off for Tantonville, our friends again imploring us not to be rash as we took leave.

On getting home, we found that Walmsley and the second raid had all returned safely but that no other machines from the First had been seen. I must say that I was a little disappointed by my reception.

'Hullo Willie, why the hell did you land at Luxeuil?'

'To get petrol sir.'

'You should ha' come straight back.'

'I had been up for five hours, and …'

'All right, Willie, mind you come straight home another time!'

Later in the day we heard that Andrews and Todd, his observer, had been killed, their machine having crashed in mysterious circumstances near Besançon; the others had forced landed all over the country.

Although the feud over Roger was officially at an end, an F.E. attacked one of our tenders, which was taking a party of officers to Nancy. Captain Puckridge, who was sitting next to the driver, received a direct hit, a large hole being burnt in his British Warm by a Verey light.

One evening Norton and I went out for a long tramp. There was nothing unusual about this, nor did we meet with adventure; yet I like to remember the frost in the air and hard dry road along which we marched to Xirocourt, across the river to Madon and over the hill to Gripport, in the valley of the Moselle.

From Gripport we made our way to the country town of Charmes, returning over the hills. The sun had set, but in the far distance we could see the tops of the Alps still glowing in its light. This supremely lovely sight held us both spellbound for some moments, but we still had some way to go, and it was too cold to stay still for long.

At Xirocourt we met a party from the squadron and joined them at dinner in the Inn. As we all walked home, we could see the flashes of anti-aircraft shells high above the horizon in the direction of the Line.

For several days we had been standing by to go to Mannheim with Captain Silly. As I was orderly officer, I was called at dawn by the guard; having put on my British Warm, I went out to 'inspect' the weather. The sky was clear, except for clouds lying along the Vosges. The air was wonderfully still and cold; shivering I went to call Gray; on hearing my report, he sprang out of bed, telling me to go and call the others.

The clouds over the Vosges made me extremely doubtful as to whether the show would be able to cross; so, wishing to be tactful, I woke one and all with the formula – 'You had better get up, but I'm not sure we shall go, it's rather dud.' For a long time Walmsley would repeat this amid general laughter.

We dressed and had breakfast, but the weather was not improving; however, the show was not cancelled, so the machines were got out, the observers tested their guns in the wood behind the hangars, and the pilots put on their Sidcots. My Sidcot had belonged to Captain Stevens, who led the first Mannheim show on Christmas Eve.

Feeling somewhat braver in all my 'war paint', I joined a little group of flying officers to await the final decision of the gods, who took council apart. Presently Farrington came towards us, 'We are going, gentlemen, you can start up now.'

I climbed into my high seat, my engine sprang into life as soon as I turned the self-starter; Bradly was already in his place. Farrington was taxiing out, followed by his raid, their engines roaring, their mechanics pushing and pull-ing as they sank into the soft ground. I ran up my engine, watching the needle of the rev. counter creep round; the light machine trembled as a thing of life to that glorious full-throated roar.

As I throttled down, Farrington came racing past up the aerodrome, old Beater, his observer, standing up in his gun ring; then Walmsley and the others left the ground in quick succession.

Our leader was now going out, so I followed quickly for I hated having mechanics dragging my wings. Once in position there was nothing to do but watch the others. One machine got badly stuck; the C.O. and Roger went to see what could be done; all the men were put on to lift and push, the engine roared, caps blew off on the mighty blast, and she came forward with a rush.

The moment I saw Silly's machine begin to move, I opened out my engine and away we raced. Hardly bothering to climb to 9,000 feet, our leader took us straight over at Blamont, and we immediately came under intense A.A. fire. I had never experienced anything quite so bad before.

I look away from the leader to the machines behind, they all in good formation; my observer is scanning the blue sky; Archy is bursting with a sound of slamming doors, black puffs of curling smoke spring into being close beside us. On we go, the sound of bursting H.E. rising every few seconds above the roar of our engine; surely this cannot last. I look round again, and see our stately machines still coming on, half hidden at times by smoke; surely someone will get hit. Behind us a long dark trail of smoke marks our path.

White bursts now appear above us, sending down streams of phosphorous all around. Somehow I do not fully realize our own danger, but expect every moment to see one of the others become unstuck'; so reads part of a letter I wrote at the time.

There must have been quite a picturesque side to all this, the twelve de Havillands over the forest-clad mountains in their two formations, with streams of glittering fireballs falling around them, in the bright sunshine of the higher regions, but I was too thoroughly alarmed to appreciate this at the time.

The weather over the Rhine looked anything but promising, but Silly kept straight on, turning neither for Archy nor cloud.

Presently we left the Vosges, and sailed peacefully above the white fog, which filled the Rhine Valley. Great cloud-mountains rising to immense altitudes now blocked our way. There, away to the right, down through a gap in the fog, or low cloud, which covered most of the floor, a canal could just be seen down in the darkness.

Silly was now partly hidden in the misty edges of cloud, then I drew away a little for fear of a collision, as he became entirely lost to view; presently I caught sight of him again, a shadow in the cloud-fog. We all kept together as well as we could through mists and sheets of rain, but at last our leader was obliged to turn back.

I was sorry, for I should have preferred a visit to Mannheim in the shelter of the clouds to going back across the open and landing with bombs. Surely Silly would take us home another way, so as to avoid those particularly unpleasant Archy batteries? No, straight back towards Zabern we go, at the same leisurely mile-a-minute gait. My heart sank as I watched those forbidding mountains, should we ever get across?

Black smoke breaks out of the void on my high left, then another and another, to the sound of drays upsetting loads of stones. It is the same all over again. I keep well forward with the leader, hoping that he will take the hint and increase his speed; but no, he sits there, complacently smiling up at me from time to time, without altering his pace or direction, in spite of intense A.A. fire.

At last we left those horrid hills, and sailed gently down to our aerodrome. Landing with bombs was always a nasty business, especially in soft ground. I think we might well have unloaded onto one of the large German camps over which we passed, but by the grace of God, we all got down safely.

Presently I met Silly. 'I'm sorry we had to turn back, chaps,' he said, rubbing his hands, 'we kept jolly good formation in those clouds, but it was quite impossible to go on.'

'Archy was heavy, sir,' I ventured.

'Yes, but the old Hun could not break up our formation,' he chuckled. I went to take off my Sidcot feeling highly pleased, yet worried by the discovery that the squadron had so little respect for shellfire.

Next morning, the weather having improved somewhat, we again set off for Mannheim. As on the previous day, we made a wide sweep to the southeast; then, turning north, we reached the Lines at Badonviller, with Farrington and co. high above, ready to cross with us should we try for Mannheim.

The Rhine Valley was still choked with fog, so our leader decided to make for Trier. Flying along the Line past Lunéville and Nancy, in full view of the enemy, we crossed at Nomeny. Archy immediately got our height, and we had a hot time until we had passed over Metz. Our progress was slow against the wind, which made matters worse, but there was no phosphorous stuff, so that I do not think I was quite so frightened as I had been the day before.

I knew that the valley of the Moselle, down which we were flying, was full of important iron works, which would be likely to be protected by A.A. guns, as well as such places as Metz and Thionville, where the barrage was intense. There seemed little prospect, therefore, of any relief from shellfire, which was not only extremely unpleasant in itself but also gave our position to any scouts that might be up after us.

Looking up, I saw steam coming from Farrington's radiator; a moment later he turned back with his raid. In spite of the fact that he had been hit by Archy, and that his engine must soon seize up, he calmly bombed the railway junction at Metz on his way home.

On and on we went, yet always more shells would burst around us. The winding Moselle now lay a little to our left, with the smoke of iron foundries rising high into the air; to our right was the wooded country of Lorraine, with the dark pine forests of the Northern Vosges beyond.

Archy had now stopped, and its absence made me uneasy, until Bradly signalled that there were a few enemy machines well below us; I had expected them to be above our height.

Now we are crossing the Saar; the wind is still fairly strong, but we shall soon be there; I wonder if the barrage will be heavy. Up goes Silly's white signal light, making a graceful curve of smoke as it falls just in front of our deputy leader. Yes, there is Trier right enough.

Approaching from the southeast, we turn westwards; I gaze anxiously around, but on seeing no Huns, turn my attention to my bomb site. At first only fields, then the outlying houses appear. I glance at the leader just as his bombs drop leisurely away from beneath him, slowly putting their noses down and gathering speed until they are lost to sight, tiny hurrying red-brown specks dashing earthwards.

We are certainly over the railway, more bombs are going down; Wild swings over rather close to me, he is probably taking aim and not looking where he is going, I must look out. Now for the goods yard, it is fully in view; I catch hold of my bomb release and tug; now for the other, I can't be too quick – I think I felt them both go but look round to Bradly for confirmation, he smiles and nods.

'Two?' I signal, 'Yes, two,' he answers.

Bombs are still falling from the other machines, I do not like to watch them go, for shells are bursting around us, and I realise for a moment that I am in a frail machine, which may be blown to matchwood at any instant: I will not consider the laws of gravity.

A phosphorous bomb is wasting its sweetness in a field some way short of the town, but its smoke shows plainly that the wind will be in our favour on the homeward journey. There are some nice brown bursts on the railway station. A thick haze of barrage smoke is hanging over the town behind us; surely the scouts will see it, if they are anywhere near; I had better keep a sharp lookout.

Archy has slackened off, and everyone is safely in his place. There is something rather deliberate about it all. We are going straight up the river again, greeted every now and then by salvos of shells from the works some 16,000 feet below. The wind is certainly helping us, we are getting on; but there may still be scouts at Thionville and Metz.

Confound that fellow! He's not looking out half enough; I draw his attention by moving my control lever, and signal ' + ?' Bradly shakes his head.

We are passing Thionville slightly to our left. Palmer is standing up in his cockpit, I wonder if he has seen anything; no, he is waving to another observer.

Hurrah! We are already passing Metz on our left, but those bursts were close, by Jove.

There are shell holes in those woods: we must be getting near the Line; I long to increase my speed but cannot, as the leader will not alter his.

A few straggling lines of trenches through the woods, and a barren strip of shelled area away to the right; a last salvo of A.A. fire, then peace; we are across.

It is now that I realise that my feet are aching with cold, I want to take them from the rudder bar and stamp them on the floor; I am thoroughly uncomfortable.

Silly is dropping below, so I pull back my throttle and altitude corrector, the note of my engine subsides into a murmur in my accustomed ears; it has never given me a moment's anxiety, I had almost forgotten that it could!

We drop down over the Forest of Haye, past Nancy. How friendly everything looks, rivers and canals shining in the sunshine, the whole country smiling to welcome us back.

What is that D.H. doing down there? The formation has got badly scattered. Never mind, there is our little brown mud-patch under Mount Zion; we shall soon be home.

I follow Silly, and watch him land; it looks from above as if he is too low; surely he will hit those trees? No, he skims safely into the aerodrome and lands, pulling up opposite the French hangar, perhaps waiting for mechanics to help him in. I circle round watching for the signal to land; there it goes. I shut off my engine and swing in over the trees and high-tension cables. As I touch I feel the mud gripping my wheels and tailskid, so pull back my controls and open the throttle; my mechanics run beside me smiling cheerfully.

News came through that evening that Fox was to go to Mannheim with the raids next day while Silly, who had been with the squadron for more than ten months, was to return to Home Establishment. Collett, who had had extra leave on account of his brother's death while flying in England, now took over the second raid from Farrington.

3

SOLO PHOTOGRAPHY

A weather reconnaissance machine reported that conditions were unchanged next morning; the Rhine Valley was still full of fog. I think we were all somewhat relieved that there was no question of Mannheim after the tiring journey of the previous day.

For the ordinary flying officers, these raids were simply unpleasant experiences; there was nothing for the pilots to do but keep in formation for several hours under shellfire, the actual dropping of the bombs being our only recreation; for the observer there was nothing but the constant watch for enemy machines. For both, in fact, there was little else to do but wonder if they would get home again.

Very different was the case of the flight commander in charge of the show, whose mind was occupied with such vital matters as speed, time, wind, height and direction. Besides this I had been badly frightened by the shellfire we had encountered, and it was with a heart-sinking feeling that I now prepared for the day's adventure; once comfortably seated in my 'office', however, my spirits rose; as always my machine restored my confidence.

Fox took us straight over at Nomeny. There was no wind, and the course followed was further from the river, so that Archy was not nearly so bad as it had been the day before.

Crossing the river soon after passing Thionville, we approached our objective from the southwest. The Zeppelin shed showed up very clearly; someone dropped a bomb, but unfortunately missed it by a few yards. White, whose engine was not pulling very well, was now flying directly beneath the formation, where he narrowly escaped destruction from falling bombs, which were being dropped on the railway station west of the river.

As we turned across the Moselle, I actually saw the flash of a bomb bursting on a large building on the right bank. Meanwhile the A.A. barrage was not particularly accurate.

Having been one of the first to drop my bombs, I now had time to notice the effects of our visit; from 15,000 feet these were not very remarkable, although fires had broken out in the vicinity of the railway station. Several bombs had fallen into the river.

On leaving the objective our formation was somewhat scattered, while the second raid had been left well behind. Archy suddenly ceased, I looked round for the cause; there on our left front were five little machines racing to meet us; I signalled to Bradly to fire his red light.

Wild and I were flying wing-tip to wing-tip with Fox; our three observers stood ready at their guns, I felt perfect confidence in their ability to beat off an attack but wondered how it would fare with our scattered machines behind. Bradly levelled his Lewis and fired as the scouts swung past us, but they did not turn until they were behind our rearmost people. We could now see the streams of white tracers flying from the observers' guns and the noses of the

Huns, but we were not able to take part, as our machines were directly between us and the foe. Had they been in their places, our rear machines would have been protected by our fire. Presently the enemy left us as suddenly as he had come.

Once more Jove sent a favourable breeze, and the Lines were soon in sight. As I sailed down towards the aerodrome the misty air seemed positively crowded with D.H.4s waiting to land, I was surprised to see Van der Riet dash in front of me, for as deputy leader, his turn was last but one. Carrol, his observer, had been slightly wounded in the scrap, so that he was quite justified in taking my place.

Another machine, with Ross and Hewitt on board, was missing, while Collett had had a narrow escape. An air lock in his petrol system had disclosed itself shortly after leaving Trier. Having lost much height, he had at last been able to restart his engine, and return to our Lines, without being seen by the scouts.

Orders for the following day were again for Mannheim, but Bradly and I were to carry out photographic reconnaissance on the Ramillies-Saarburg area, south of Trier. We were given a list of objects, and spent some time studying our maps, while *No. 6* had her fresh set of bombs removed and oxygen cylinders fitted.

Next morning the raids set off once more for Mannheim. As soon as they had gone, I had my machine taken from the hangar; I was feeling exceedingly anxious, for I knew that the whole of my future career in the squadron might depend on the success of this flight.

I climbed from the wet ground to my comfortable seat, wiping off the mud from my boots on the huge tyres as I did so. Bradly was listening to the last exhortations of Sticky, the photographic officer.

We crossed at 20,000 in well under the hour, and, flying over Delme, reached our objective in the neighbour-hood of Ramillies in exceedingly misty weather. It was just possible to see the ground directly below, whilst now and then we caught the gleam of water in the distance, and the white salt-lake at Château-Salins, which already seemed very far away, yet beyond it again lay the Line. Just as I realised this, I caught sight of a patrol of Huns flying southeast in the direction of Metz at 18,000 feet, but my double Vickers gave me confidence and I continued to circle, taking photographs.

The presence of five enemy machines between us and the Line was very distracting, however, and I had to keep one eye continually on their movements. I thought at first that they would be able to climb to our height, and wondered as we took each picture whether we should have time to take another before beating a retreat.

We were now at 21,000, while the enemy must have been quite 2,000 feet below, though it did not appear so at the time. Thus they followed us from place to place as we did our work, hoping that we might suffer from engine trouble and so fall an easy prey to their twin Spandau guns.

Now and then, between the objectives, Bradly would get up from his camera, take careful aim and rattle off a few shots, while I looked on with intense interest. Unfortunately, after watching one of these little diversions, I discovered that I no longer knew where I was. The mist had grown even thicker, and the railway, which I had been following, was now nowhere to be seen.

The enemy presently gave up the game, being quite unable to reach our height, while I flew by compass in the direction of Saarburg. Owing to the position of the sun, it was impossible to see the ground in front; the little we could see lay to the northwest and gave no indication of our position, being nothing but a mass of woods.

After a long and fruitless search for our remaining objectives, we were obliged by lack of petrol to make for home. On crossing the Lines I signalled to Bradly to take a photograph so that we might learn later where we had been, for I was very uncertain as to our position. Soon after this I formed a pretty good idea as to where we were and was able to reach Tantonville without further trouble.

On landing I found that Bradly was suffering from frostbite. The raids had been to Pirmasens. That night we again went to bed early, the weather report being good, but awoke to hear the blessed drip of rain.

'What a depressing morning!' remarked Lady Di, who did not fly; he narrowly escaped with his life.

After breakfasting at 9:30, we strolled up to the hangars, where mechanics were at work cleaning and overhauling our faithful mounts; my rigger was busily removing the mud, which had been thrown up by my tyres onto the under surface of my lower planes, while my fitter inspected one of my four magnetos.

Presently I came across the technical sergeant major, and we talked about old days at Lilbourne.

'It was a pity you ever left the squadron, Sir,' he remarked, 'we were talking in the mess the other night, and we said you would have had a flight by now if you had come out with us.'

'Oh well, you can't tell, I might have been killed by now Sergeant Major.'

'Oh no, Sir, you haven't been killed, so you wouldn't have been killed.' This fatalism struck me as being eminently suitable for an airman, and I tried to adopt much the same attitude.

Sammy now joined me, and we walked into the damp behind the hangars, first to the gun room to enquire into the cause of a stoppage he had had with his Vickers, then to Head Quarters Workshops to see if there was any more three-ply wood for map boards; and so to Sticky's Photographic Section.

Here Crane was found discussing yesterday's plates with several officers. Metior was discovered warming himself over a stove, and trying to explain why his weather report had been so hopelessly wrong to a few sarcastic friends. It then struck me that my electrical foot-warmers were out of order, so we went to Miller's Equipment Stores to change them. At each of these ports of call we were received with the greatest civility and good humour; after all, we were the only raison d'être for all these departments.

The rain lasted for some days, by no means continuously, but the state of the aerodrome combined with clouds right down on the hilltops and bad visibility put all work out of the question.

Football was now much to the fore; we had some good inter-flight games, and the squadron defeated a number of French units in the neighbourhood. The latter, although they invariably indulged in mutual recriminations directly we scored, were clean players.

A definite run was marked out for officers who would not, or could not, play football; several of us joined regularly in both, so we got a certain amount of exercise, but I failed to get a place in the Squadron Eleven.

Recreation was also to be had in the form of trips to Nancy, but the seats in the tender were always monopolised by the younger members of the squadron, who appeared anxious to have a gay time; I could, no doubt, have claimed a place, but I had found that even the briefest contact with civilisation tended to undermine my resolution to succeed at all costs.

Meanwhile I found the delay somewhat tiresome – 'I want to complete the trip I began the other day,' I wrote, 'I wonder if my Hun friends will be there to escort me round again. I am afraid I am suffering from an attack of over confidence and fatalism; but that is better than the ungodly fear I always had before.

After all, the work has to be done, and so long as my machine and her crew are in the highest state of efficiency possible, it is no good worrying. Of course a lucky bullet or H.E. might finish the best of 'gasoline-kites'; but that is beyond our control.

It is rather sad to look round our big mess, and wonder how many of the fellows will be sitting there in three months' time, for I expect it will be a case of '*Adieu, la très gentile compagnie!*'

On the following Sunday Emma Gee took us for a practice formation, as the weather had improved somewhat. A number of French people in their pretty national costumes came up to watch the flying after Mass. Some small boys, who walked across the aerodrome at the peril of their lives, were captured and shut up in the guardroom until flying was over.

Orders were now posted for the raids to go to Mainz, with Farrington leading, while I was to complete the Saarburg – Ramillies reconnaissance and then go on to the Boulay – St. Avold area. I was told, quite unofficially, that if I managed to do this photography before the raids were able to go, I should be given a place in preference to one of the new pilots.

On 27 February we were all called, as the weather had cleared, but the aerodrome was in a terrible condition, and the bombers were unable to reach their starting positions through the mud, so that the show had to be washed out.

Meanwhile Fluke and I had everything ready, so that we could start off in the squadron's new '375', a D.H.4. fitted with the latest type of Rolls, which developed this horse power, as soon as the hard-worked mechanics could turn their attention to us.

I had now become so accustomed to *No. 6*, that I felt quite strange in this machine. A little crowd collected to watch us start; Fluke climbed into his place; I ran up the engine, it was not very smooth; but there was such a feeling of power in that mighty rush of air, that all fear was swept away. Impatient of the ground, I raced straight up the aerodrome, the machine taking off with ease, in spite of the mud. A quick climbing turn, back over the hangars, then a steady climb away southwards.

The single Vickers failed to give me much sense of security; surely this machine was very draughty? Or was it because we were alone? No, the engine was not running smoothly; never mind, we were fast gaining our height.

Fourteen thousand, time to swing north again. Those fields are badly flooded – Hullo! She doesn't take much extra air – risk of fire with those blow-backs – Ugh! If we caught alight up here – I think I had better take a little oxygen, it will make me feel braver.

She's getting cooler now: I can open full out. Fifteen-five; there is the aerodrome, I wonder if they can see us. I don't suppose Fluke has ever been more than 17,000 feet before,

I hope he'll be all right, supposing he was to faint and fall on his controls? I wonder if we shall see those Huns again –

Heavens! What was that? A bump at fifteen-five? Funny things are happening today, I hope nothing vital is breaking. Time is slipping by, and we are not at the Lines by any means; well, we shall have a very strong north wind in our favour coming home.

Temperature 83, let me see, that means she's pretty hot, you add a degree for every 1,000 feet; I think she'd climb better at 70. Oh, I know what those bumps were: of course, it's Fluke jumping about in his cockpit. Silly of me to be so frightened; how the others would laugh if they knew how timid I am!

The Alps are lovely! '*Salu hauteurs sublimes, Vous qui montez aux cieux!*'

Did you hear that little croak? That was my top note above the roar of the engine. I do not think I will sing any more, that croak frightened me, making me realise how small and weak I am.

That is the same field I noticed just now, the wind must be extremely strong up here; never mind, we are climbing well, 18,000 and she doesn't feel a bit soggy yet.

On and up we go, lifted imperceptibly, as if by magic, into a bluer heaven, into sunshine of more dazzling brightness. The earth stretches below us, clearly marked for 10 or 15 miles, and growing less and less distinct in the hazy distance; though here a river, and there the dark mass of some wood, stands out in the mists which hide the horizon.

Behind us float the Alps, floating like swans above the brown waters of some vast lake, so completely detached from earth they seem. What a glorious scene, how I could enjoy it, if only fear were not tugging at my heart – 'Will you ever get back? Perhaps you will run into those Huns – you would not have a hope against three or four – What would it be like if –' I had better take some more oxygen, it will cheer me up.

I gaze out forward, a few light clouds detach themselves from the mists, come hurrying to meet us, and are passed. There is Lunéville aerodrome; how absurdly close to the Line, but then those damned Frenchmen have got an arrangement with the Hun not to bomb each other's aerodromes. Not a machine to be seen; perhaps that is just as well, one might get shot up by the Nieuports.

Nineteen thousand; this is mysterious, not a shell from Archy; I wonder if their scouts are about, I must get Fluke to have a good look round. Those are their trenches below that we are over.

The well-known Salt Lake of Château-Salins lies to the right; in front of us is the mallet-shaped Forêt de Ramillies, where lies our first objective, the aerodrome at Han, near the junction of the two railways at the end of the handle.

The engine was not running at all smoothly and was much hotter than I liked, so I throttled down a little.

Just as we were about to fly over Han, in order to take our photographs, I caught sight of four machines coming towards us at about 16,000 feet, from the direction of Metz; this naturally increased my anxiety for my engine. I felt sure they must have seen us; for I always imagined, when flying, that half the sky was filled by my own broad wings and that everyone within 20 miles must be watching our stately progress.

From Han we flew up the Metz–St Avold line, taking other aerodromes on the way. Progress was slow against the wind, which appeared to be north-easterly at 20,000 feet; but St Avold soon lay close in front, nestling under its woods. Our four scouts still flew due east at 17,000 feet, away on our right, little black specks fading away in the mists of the moisture-laden atmosphere.

Our troubles were only beginning, however; Fluke, whose work demanded a certain amount of physical exertion, which would in any case have been exhausting at this height, was now suffering from failure of his oxygen. I therefore made all possible speed to reach Sarre-Union and finish the work.

The heavy smoke of Saarbrucken lay on the left; in the haze on our right the Ponds of Lorraine gleamed with an ominous, unfriendly light amid the dark woods. Somewhere between us and the Line flew the four Huns.

Fluke managed to photograph the aerodrome at Sarre-Union, then fainted. At the same moment my engine began to show unmistakable signs of distress, steam began to pour from the radiator, and the vibration became very marked, so I headed straight for home.

I had throttled back the engine; but the vibration was so violent that I presently thought it safer to switch off. I knew that I had plenty of height to reach the Line, if only I did not run into the enemy, for I had a strong following wind.

Keeping a very sharp lookout, and travelling at what I considered to be the machine's best gliding angle, I made my way southwest towards the nearest point of friendly territory. Suddenly I caught sight of the four little scouts, high up in the clear blue sky to my right. I immediately 'executed a turning way movement' to the left. On looking round I still could not see Fluke, who was in the bottom of his cockpit; we were completely defenceless.

Fortunately, the scouts did not see us and presently they faded once more from sight. We were now down at 14,000, and I began to think that Fluke must be dead, but at length he was able to stand up again.

We expected to be heavily shelled at the Line, but thanks to the mist, and the fact that our engine was silent, Archy did not see us until we were crossing.

I thought, at first, of landing at Lunéville, but as we still had 10,000 feet in hand, I decided to make for home. We arrived at Tantonville with plenty of height to spare, and landed comfortably in the middle of the aerodrome.

It was found that a piston had been blown in, a very extraordinary cause of failure. Our long glide home was mentioned in 'Comic Cuts', the Flying Corp's Official Bulletin, as a record.

4

MAINZ, STUTTGART AND COBLENZ

Morning broke with uncertain prospects; it was true that the raids had not been called, but there was neither rain nor fog. After breakfast I went up to the hangars with Bradly, who had now recovered sufficiently from the frostbite to be ready for a further attempt to complete the Saarburg and district aerodrome reconnaissance, before the raids could go to Mainz.

Low clouds everywhere, there would be no photography today; anyhow, it was just as well to see that *No. 6* was absolutely ready.

Presently I met Farrington and Collett, the latter was going to Nancy with Miller and Jones; would I like to go too? My French would be useful in the market, where Miller bought provisions for the mess. No, Farrington thought there was no hope of the weather clearing.

We were soon whirring along the road, Miller and I suffering somewhat from the draught, which always blew into the back of a closed tender. However, we were soon hooting our way through busy streets, thronged with soldiers and civilians of every description.

Marketing proved rather a tame business; Miller, who was apparently very well known, had been unduly modest with regard to his French, and there was absolutely no bargaining. As we walked back to the Crossley, followed by our driver, who was laden with parcels, we caught sight of a little boy of 8 or 9 wearing a large white bandage round his head; on being asked if he had had an accident, he told us that he had been wounded during an air raid a few nights previously. He did not beg, but we all felt so angry with 'Those bloody Huns' for doing such things, that we gave him a number of Francs.

It may have occurred to us that children in Germany were suffering in like manner through our own mistaken aim, but I simply refused to consider the possibility. To me, Germany represented a huge fighting machine, which we were bound to resist with every means in our power, if we were not to be crushed.

An excellent lunch at the Restaurant Stanislaus was sadly disturbed by the appearance of the sun, which lit up the historic Square with its wintry light. Presently I could stand it no longer, and asked Collett if we might return to the aerodrome with all possible speed. He seemed rather amused by my anxiety, and assured me that it was only a local 'hot air patch', most probably due to an up-draught from Wing H.Q. Besides, Farrington had said that the weather was unfit for photography.

Presently the sun went in again. We afterwards did a little shopping, chiefly consisting of articles bearing the double cross of Lorraine, and enjoyed the most luxurious hot baths at the Hotel d'Angleterre.

I sat with Collett in front going home, but I fear I was not a very entertaining companion as I was still obsessed with the idea that I had missed a golden opportunity.

It was not until 6 March that the weather cleared sufficiently for a show, but once more the raids were unable to get off, owing to the mud. Having watched the flounderings of these unfortunate people with secret satisfaction, I set off with Bradly in *No. 6*. It was very pleasant to be back in my own machine; after all, the engine developed 320 horsepower, and I felt that I could give a good account of myself with my twin Vickers.

We had a most interesting and successful flight, discovering a number of new aerodromes, and taking photos at Bühl, Saarburg, Bensdorf, Morhange and Many, amongst other places. We saw no enemy machines at our height, and *No. 6* ran perfectly, climbing to 22,000 feet before we recrossed the Lines on our way home.

That evening both Wing and Brigade rang up to congratulate us, but the discovery that fresh aerodromes were being built on our Front was not reassuring.

No. 6 was now to fly deputy leader to Collett, who was leading the second raid to Mainz, her load being increased by two phosphorous bombs, in addition to the usual '112s'. Bradly insisted on coming with me, in spite of renewed frostbite; that night we had another map festival, as I was determined not to lose the way in the improbable event of our leader falling out after losing sight of the first raid.

Mainz was certainly a long way, but that was all to the good; I was tired of hearing about Mannheim, this would take the wind out of the sails of people who still talked about the show on Christmas Eve.

The aerodrome was still in a bad condition, but we all managed to get off safely, and an hour later Farrington took us over at Badonviller under ideal weather conditions.

I was too much occupied with the novelty of my position, below and behind the leader, to be able to admire the scene, but I am sure that our twelve machines in their close formations, booming along 12,000 feet above the forest-clad Vosges on that perfect morning of early spring must have been a sight not easily forgotten by the high gods.

Archy was not up to his usual form, and the few E.A. we saw were nowhere near our height. The forests became more scattered; to our left lay the smoke of Saarbrucken, to our right the Rhine grew more distant, with Karlsruhe beyond.

The sky now became overcast with a high white covering, greatly above us; we flew in the chasm between earth and sky, in pale, strained sunshine.

Shall we meet the scouts from Mannheim? I wish those fellows would keep up closer. Ludwigshafen is already on our right, the smoke of its factories hanging over it like a pall; we are passing safely. Just think: we are over 100 miles from the Line. We are being left behind by Fifi, who sits away there in front. Diana 3 is too darned slow; Collett should get a new bus.

Let me see, that must be Darmstadt away down there. On and on we go, constantly watching the sky for enemies who do not appear.

Great Scott! What are all those machines streaming across our bows? Hun two-seaters? No, it's only Fifi and his crowd, but where are they off to? We must be nearly there now; I must have an extra good look round.

Collett did not follow Farrington, as our objective was the railway from Frankfort, on the east side of the town. The barrage was for the most part below our height, which was now 15,500 feet, but a number of bursts were unpleasantly close.

As we turned south above the broad river with its many barges, Farrington came racing by in the opposite direction. Several E.A. were now sighted, but I think they had only taken the air for greater safety from our bombs; in any case, they made no attempt to attack us.

Our formation had now become hopelessly scattered, *No. 6* alone remaining with Collett, who headed straight for home. On looking back I saw several D.H.4s still circling in the barrage over Mainz, but the first raid was nowhere to be seen.

I religiously maintained my position just under Diana's tailskid, although there was not another machine in sight; possibly this would have been the safest place for me if we had been attacked. I think the danger of a scout getting into a blind spot under the tail was much exaggerated, I never saw a machine shot down by this method; a straight, determined dive, however, often proved fatal, either to attacker or attacked.

Presently we saw two scouts away east at 16,000, but they did not approach, and a little later Farrington caught us up with ten machines, his own raid and our stragglers. I was thankful to see them, as I thought we were certain to meet with opposition on the way home.

My engine was running with its usual monotonous perfection, but should we have enough petrol to get home? I tried to make calculations, but could not do the simplest mental arithmetic under these conditions, so gave it up and watched Diana's tailskid swinging slowly above my head.

The rest of the journey was completely devoid of incident, as the enemy failed to interfere with us, except, of course, by means of A.A. guns. Everyone was delighted at Farrington's success, but the pilots who left their places, owing to their anxiety to make good shots with their bombs, were well and truly strafed.

That night we drank our leader's health in weak French beer, the weather report holding good. Orders were up for Stuttgart, with Farrington leading, Thakrah having the second raid.

I was dead tired when called next morning, and I expect the others were too, although I do not remember hearing anyone say so. We of the second raid were to take off first, and we were all in position on the green strip of grass down the centre of the aerodrome. As soon as Thakrah began to move, one of his bombs fell off; quickly the thought flashed through my mind that I was fairly safe behind my engine, even if it exploded; then, as it failed to do so, I followed, taking good care to keep well to the right of the yellow projectile. As I reached the top of the rise, I saw that the Frenchmen had dragged out one of their aeroplanes right into my path; I managed, however, to miss it by a few feet by raising my machine.

I did not realise at the moment what a narrow escape I had had, but went on my way consigning our Allies, and their bird cage, to eternal punishment. I am sorry to say that my imprudent take off sadly upset the nerves of those about to follow.

We were soon flying just below Thakrah, his tailskid swinging above us a few yards away; every now and then a few bits of grass would fall from it into space, while his big wheels on his long undercarriage seemed to be groping for the ground which was no longer there: one of them was still going round very slowly, and I watched it, wondering vaguely whether it would ever turn on our aerodrome again.

Presently Rayment, Thakrah's observer, swung his gun-mounting round and looked over the side.

On looking down, I saw that we were going south, then swinging east over the Forêt de Charmes; I wished our leader would keep away from the Line until we were ready to cross, it was quite unnecessary to advertise the fact that we were coming an hour beforehand, but he did not seem to care whether the Hun knew or not.

Farrington was climbing swiftly with his raid, while our people lagged behind. We circled several times between Charmes and the Vosges, finally Fifi slipped across just when Bumps was at the farthest point of the orbit from the Line. Thakrah now dashed after the first raid, with our formation in a very scattered condition, only *No. 6* being able to keep her place.

Archy was bursting round Farrington's compact little formation above us, away to the northeast. The shell smoke looked so black and solid in the clear sky, that I mistook it at first for E.A. All this I saw in a semi dozing condition.

Whrumph! A shell burst very close to me, I woke up suddenly, ugh! We are really going over, God help us!

My goggles were partly frosted over; I thought I saw more E.A. I shivered with fright and cold – 'Come, this will never do, a deputy leader must not give way to foolish fears,' I thought, and immediately felt happier.

The usual fireworks followed; we always got phosphorous Archy over that part of the Vosges. Thakrah altered his course frequently, in order to puzzle the gunners, while Farrington appeared to keep straight on; presently the first raid was but a group of tiny brown specks, followed by a long trail of smoke, far away, high up in the limpid blue.

The ground now sank some thousands of feet down to the Rhine Valley; once clear of the Vosges Archy, Bumps straightened his course and hurried forward again, in order to keep Farrington in sight.

Many miles to the north we could see the barrage floating above Karlsruhe; it was amusing to think that for 30 miles on either side of our course the Huns were spending this lovely morning in damp cellars, imagining from the noise of their own guns that their towns were the object of our attack.

Farrington was now being shelled above the Rhine, and presently we too crossed the mighty river:

Es braust ein Ruf im Himmel blau,
Wo Heldengeister nieder schauen,
Zum Rhein, zum Rhein, zum Deutschen Rhein!
Wo alle wollen Hütter sein!

The call of twelve Rolls engines in the blue sky remained unanswered, for not one defender could we see. How peaceful Lahr looks down there, nestling against the sombre mass of the Black Forest. Would there be more A.A. fire from those peaks? Yes, Farrington was getting a few bursts. Ten minutes later Bradly pulled the communication cord, which I had tied to my left arm, and signalled that we were followed by enemy machines; on looking round, I saw that he had mistaken three of our own machines, which had been left far behind, for Huns! Sansom, Brookes and Gavaghan were badly handicapped by their slow machines. This very gallant trio all lost their lives in subsequent shows because they could not keep up.

Over Freudenstadt, and so to the river Neckar, which we followed for the remainder of the journey to Stuttgart. Everything was wonderfully peaceful; we might almost have been flying over part of England as we passed over several pleasant-looking towns.

Time was getting on; Stuttgart was away to the north, while we were still flying due east; had Farrington lost his way? No, that was impossible. I vaguely wondered if he was going to try for Dresden. This town was not on my maps, being too far east, and I had no idea how far it was, but the thought of Farrington being taken prisoner, through lack of petrol, was as grotesque as that of his losing his way. I had perfect confidence in our leader, and felt that it was almost a sin to worry.

We now followed the wide sweep of the river from northeast to northwest; this gave the stragglers a much-needed opportunity to cut across and regain us, while we, in our turn, were able to catch up with the first raid.

Contrary to our usual practice, and in spite of our experience on the previous day, each pilot had been given his own particular target, mine being the Daimler Works at Untertürkheim, a suburb southeast of the town; my bombs fell on the railway sidings beside the factory, setting a train on fire.

Meanwhile Bradly began to take photographs. We were now flying through the heavy barrage over the town, our formation being badly scattered, owing to the fact that each machine was looking for its own objective.

We were just getting clear of the shellfire, when something made me glance up over my left shoulder; a scout was coming down on me out of the sun, not 300 yards away. I immediately pulled my machine up in a climbing turn to the left, to avoid his bullets. The scout pilot came out of his dive, overshooting me as he did so; then he went straight down from a beautiful half-roll, being frightened away, it would seem, by the sight of our markings.

Meanwhile Bradly was still in the bottom of his cockpit taking photographs. I had exactly the sensation one gets when one finds a wasp in the jam one was about to put in one's mouth, but I could not help admiring both the smooth way in which the pilot handled his machine and its beautiful condition. 'Being a smaller machine, it is not difficult for the Rigger to clean the top of her planes,' I thought.

Owing to the presence of several E.A. our people closed up their ranks more quickly than they had at Mainz, but Thackrah was setting too hot a pace for our slower machines, so I throttled down slightly in order to allow them to keep with me; our observers concentrated a hot fire on any scout that came within range, but the enemy showed neither skill nor courage, and completely failed to press the attack.

Farrington was now high up in front of the second raid. Presently another flight of scouts came diving to meet us. One fellow came right through Farrington's formation, then straight down on us. Turning under Thakrah's tail, he pulled up his nose and began to shoot; I immediately got him in my Aldis sight and fired.

I had climbed a little when waiting for our rear machines so now came down on the intruder at a great pace, with my engine full on, and both my guns going. I could see my tracers striking the fuselage, and passing through the wings of the scout, a fascinating sight!

When but a few yards from the E.A. I saw it fall over on one side, and disappear, the next instant I was climbing and turning past Thakrah. The scout was last seen going straight down in a vertical dive some thousands of feet below our formation.

With one honourable exception, the enemy had shown no desire to make our close acquaintance. Several scouts sat high up behind us, waiting for someone to fall out of formation. Presently I was distressed to see that Caldicott, the nearest machine in Farrington's formation, was in difficulties; steam was coming from his radiator, and his propeller was going round very slowly.

We passed quite close to this unfortunate machine, both pilot and observer waving to us to show that they were unwounded. I watched them glide down for a long time, fearing that the scouts would pounce on them, but they wisely kept below our formation, and were probably unobserved.

After about ten minutes the enemy left us, but time was getting on, there was a head wind, and I began to wonder if we should have enough petrol after all.

At last the edge of the Schwarzwald came in sight, and a little later the faint blue outline of the Vosges … very far away. I felt fairly certain that we should run into more Huns over the Rhine Valley; if we were delayed, we should certainly run out of petrol.

My fears proved groundless, however, for although we saw several E.A. there was no more fighting, and everyone, with the exception of Caldicott, reached the Line safely.

When the formation broke up after crossing to our side, Thakrah and I flew home together through the fine weather mist. Unfortunately, several people ran out of petrol and crashed in unsuitable country; no one was hurt, but it had been a near thing.

The squadron had a rest the next day, but there were photographs to get, so I set out with Bradly in *No. 6*. Farrington had told me that I must get all the pictures without fail, as we were going to Coblenz on the following day.

No. 6 was going great guns, so we crossed the Line at 20,000 feet in less than an hour. I missed the companion-ship of the others, but our experience at Stuttgart had given me confidence; I was beginning to realise that the Huns were a very different crowd to those I had met up north the year before.

First we flew to Metz, where we began to take photos. Archy fired a few shots at us, but they were all very wide of the mark. A big patrol of eight enemy machines passed us 2–3,000 feet below, flying in a westerly direction. They ignored us completely. We then flew to Thionville, Bettembourg, Luxembourg and Pettingen; Saarburg, Saarlouis and Saarbrucken followed, photographs being taken at all places of interest. We came back to the Line by way of Bensdorf and the Lakes.

Our reconnaissance having pleased the gods, we were given a place in the show for the following day, this time as Farrington's deputy leader.

Everyone was pleased to hear that the roof of the main station at Trier had been blown in, and that its collapse had caused the death of a number of enemy soldiers.

Poor Bradly was again suffering so badly from frostbite that he was unable to go with me next morning, so I took Sergeant Hodge, who had now returned from leave.

At first we flew above thick ground mist; very little was to be seen of the earth. I saw the high cone of rocks and stone from a mine near Nancy, sticking up through the white valley fog.

Farrington's *No. 4* was easy to follow; old Beater, his observer, kept popping his head over the side to have a look at us. As we crossed the Line, the sun was driving the mists away. Our leader took us mid way between Metz and Saarbrucken, so that we were little troubled by Archy, but we were soon passing over the wooded Eifel, which was peculiarly free from good landmarks. Our leader steered a true course, and at last, beyond the forests, I saw the sunlight reflected on a stretch of water, the Rhine. Presently I made out the winding Moselle away to the left. At the junction of the two rivers we should find Coblenz.

On reaching our objective, we ran into very heavy A.A. fire, but we got good bursts on the railway sidings. As we turned to our right above the river, we could see our second raid dropping their bombs as they ploughed their way through the barrage, while some of the effects of our own visit were plainly visible.

The monotony of the homeward journey was broken by a very half-hearted attack by a few E.A. One scout caused some excitement by diving away steeply, with black smoke pouring out behind him, but he failed to burst into flames.

5

'A CARTLOAD OF MONKEYS'

The next day we were very short of machines, as a number were in need of overhaul after the strenuous work of the past week; so the gods decided that Collett should go on the comparatively short trip to Freiburg with only nine followers, although it was the 13th. As soon as they had gone, I took off in *No. 6* to photograph a railway we had discovered under construction near Luxembourg.

Soon after crossing at Nomeny, I noticed a curious period in the engine. This sort of thing always added to my anxiety, but as the revs did not drop, nor the temperature rise, nor the oil-pressure slacken, I kept straight on at 21,000 feet.

Having taken photographs of Frescarti aerodrome, we flew high over the heads of a patrol of five scouts and took a new aerodrome, which we had noticed on our way back from Coblenz. We then went to Luxembourg, and having, as I thought, taken pictures of the new railway, proceeded to admire the town at our leisure.

I now steered a course for Verdun by way of the busy industrial area of Esche – Longuyon, taking many photos on the way. Luxembourg had been brilliantly clear, but this district was thick with smoke.

I had never been to Verdun before, but it was easily recognised, the yellow shelled area beside the Meuse being visible at a great distance.

Several E.A. were flying along the Line at but little below our height; probably they were on the lookout for Frenchmen, and looking westward; in any case, they made no attempt to interfere with us.

We crossed and enjoyed a very interesting trip up the river to the German bridgehead at St Michael. As I watched the trenches, I wondered how Collett had fared.

Sticky met us on landing and said something about Collett having lost several machines, but I was too deaf from the roar of my engine to hear him properly. Eight machines had reached the objective, but as they turned homeward they were attacked by fifteen to twenty scouts, with the result that three of our slowest machines, Wilson, Brookes and Gavaghan, were shot down.

I do not know how many casualties the enemy suffered; the squadron never believed the enthusiastic claims of new observers; in fact, it was considered almost poor taste to say that one had shot a Hun!

Ward reported that he had caused an Albatros to leave the combat in a steep dive, but he was careful to add that he felt sure it was under control.

When Sticky's people developed our photographs, it was discovered that Hodge had missed out the middle of our new railway, through changing a box of plates at the critical moment. Intelligence was much annoyed, and Wing gave orders that only officers should go on reconnaissance in future.

Although Hodge had never been posted as my observer, I felt that he had the prior right, but Gray pointed out that if I insisted on keeping him, I could neither go on photography nor be a deputy leader, for the latter's observer always had a camera. This proved unanswerable.

The next day the squadron had a rest, while I went on the Luxembourg recon in *No. 6* with Bradly; this time we were completely successful.

In the evening we all went down to the railway to help unload new machines; this was very interesting work, and made quite an agreeable change. When we got back to the mess, we found that eight new flying officers had arrived; the best people were delighted to find that two of the newcomers had double-barrelled names and possessed regiments.

One of the new pilots was called Keep; I had known him when testing, and it was nice to be able to welcome him to the squadron.

The next day, 15 March, I went on reconnaissance with Ward, as Bradly was frostbitten. Unfortunately, we found that all the country north of Metz was obscured by masses of dense cloud. We flew on in the hope of finding holes, but after half an hour's vain search, we were obliged to turn homewards.

Presently I caught sight of a formation of four E.A. climbing towards the Line; we watched them for the next ten minutes, but when they reached the trenches, they turned and flew away westward.

I crossed and began to lose height, thinking no more of the scouts. Suddenly I caught sight of French Archy going up away to the right; I immediately opened out my engine and hurried in that direction so as to see what was happening.

Presently we made out an enemy two-seater about 3 miles on our side, while the four scouts flew in a compact little group at a somewhat greater height, but at such a distance that they were, at the moment, useless as an escort.

I decided to attack the two-seater; unfortunately she saw us coming and put her nose down for the Lines before we could get close. I went down after her with my engine full on, firing several bursts in an attempt to make her turn.

Glancing round, I saw Ward standing at his gun, watching the scouts with a broad smile on his face. The two-seater was going straight down; every moment I expected the scouts to come to the rescue, but I was much too excited to be afraid of them; besides, I had absolute confidence in Ward.

We were now crossing the Line at about 8,000 feet; I had been unable to get within effective range of the enemy two-seater and knew that it would be highly imprudent to follow her too far over, on account of the scouts, so fired a long burst with both guns, hoping that a chance shot might destroy the E.A.

As I turned, I almost ran into an Albatros scout, but he dived away without firing a shot, giving Ward only the time for a short burst. I do not think this machine belonged to the very inefficient escort; probably the pilot was so surprised to see a de Havilland at 5,000 feet that he was completely unnerved.

I think our little adventure helped to restore the morale of the younger members of the squadron, who had been somewhat rattled by their experience at Freiburg.

The next day Fox set out for Mannheim, with Farrington leading the second raid, *No. 6* being the latter's deputy. Having shown ourselves at the Line soon after leaving the ground, we were met by a number of E.A. on crossing fifty minutes later.

Farrington was flying above and behind Fox, while the scouts sat up behind us at a considerable distance, with plenty of height in hand. I watched them anxiously, but they appeared to be in no hurry to attack us.

Presently Sansom, one of Fox's raid, began to be left behind in his slow machine; by the time we reached Saargemünd, he was some distance behind our formation.

Suddenly two E.A. came down on this unfortunate machine, their tracers spraying all over her, her observer firing back. I immediately swung my machine round and went down to her assistance.

The scouts both sought safety by diving, but I got my sights onto one of them and gave him a good burst with both guns. I could see my tracers striking the fuselage just behind the pilot's seat, but I could not follow him, for there were many other E.A. above me, and I had to rejoin the formation.

Realising that I had bombs, and that my airspeed indicator had got well into its second revolution – it only registered up to 160mph in the ordinary way – I allowed *No. 6* to come out of the dive very gently and raced after the raids. Several E.A. now came down on us; I turned and fired at the nearest, but he too dived away. Not wishing to lose more height, I was only able to give him quite a short burst before coming out of the dive, and hurrying after the others once more.

Presently we were climbing past Sansom's machine, and I was delighted to see both pilot and observer waving to us.

We were now escorted by a number of scouts, but they kept at a respectful distance. I wanted Ward to fire at them, but he only smiled and shook his head, they were too far away.

Five minutes later we were back in our place in formation, but my heart sank, for Sansom turned round and flew back towards the Line followed by the Huns. There was, of course, no question of going to his assistance a second time, if *No. 6* was to go to Mannheim with the show, he must be left to the wolves.

Presently we were dropping our bombs at Zweibrücken. Archy alone disturbed the peace of our homeward way. I wondered vaguely why we had turned back so soon, yet felt extremely thankful on crossing the Line, for I was due to go on leave the next day.

Coming in sight of the aerodrome, we saw a D.H. on the ground outside A Flight; had Sansom got back after all? On landing I saw that it was indeed his machine; it was badly shot about, but both he and Sergeant Ryan, his gunner, stood beside it.

As we walked down to the office, Farrington reproved me gently for leaving my place in formation; by all the rules of the game, I should have been shot down; besides what would happen to the show if everyone started to scrap with their front guns? Some of the observers were scolded for not using more ammunition.

'Not fire?' exclaimed Stewart, a young Canadian. 'Gee, they were as shy as a cartload of monkeys! Not a blamed one came near me.' Sansom said that although the E.A. had followed him back to the Line, they had been careful to keep out of range.

After tea I took up a practice formation consisting of new pilots, having for my observer a gentleman who suffered from short sight, for he had not seen, and therefore had not fired at, the enemy that morning. I went close enough to the Line to make the Hun send up some Archy on his side, whereupon my observer signalled that he saw innumerable E.A.!

When we landed, Stewart asked why I had not taken them over to look for a scrap. My chief anxiety was now for the safety of *No. 6* during my absence, but Farrington promised that she should be used as little as possible, and then only by a good pilot.

Next day Fox and Farrington again set out for Mannheim, this time to reach Kaiserslautern, while I spent my time in Nancy before catching the night express for Paris.

We stopped several times beyond Toul on account of 'Avion'; I gazed out of the window at the stars, listening to the throb of twin engines and the hiss of steam. During the night I was vaguely conscious of a long delay at Chalons-sur-Marne. Avions, it seemed, had bombed the station and done much damage.

Next day, 18 March, I travelled north with an Australian major, who told me about the great offensive that was expected on the British front during the next few days, 'God help our people in the Line when the Hun pushes,' he said.

Arrived at Boulogne, we had lunch at the officers' club and then embarked. The usual crowd of officers in lifebelts, including a goodly number of brass hats and generals, were seated on the top deck. Presently we heard the sound of guns and saw an enemy two-seater come out of the clouds at no very great height and calmly proceed to photograph the harbour.

'Look out for shrapnel!' someone shouted, but we all gazed aloft at our gallant foes. As we steamed out of harbour, the French destroyer that was to have escorted us decided that it was too rough; while a little group of R.F.C. officers who had taken up a position right in the bows, came back aft, drenched to the skin by a big wave.

Deckchairs broke loose and carried their occupants into the scuppers. No sooner had these unfortunates regained their feet, than a lurch in the opposite direction sent them running helplessly across the deck to crash into the hatches and other obstructions.

Grey seas seemed to heave high above us as we rolled, the spray flew in our faces, the wind tried to snatch off our caps, while the narrow ribbon of steam from a pipe on the funnel blew out in an eddying line. Presently a British destroyer met us and steamed alongside; at length we were safely inside Folkestone Harbour.

6

B FLIGHT

Leave passed all too quickly, and when but ten of the precious fourteen days were gone, a telegram came recalling me to the squadron. The great German offensive on the British Front had begun, and I was almost glad to go.

A taxi drive to Filton, which happened to be the nearest aerodrome, and in half an hour I was off in a brand-new Bristol Fighter, speeding through low clouds and rain.

Landing in Marquise, I met several old friends and was given a Camel to take to Saint-André au Bois. It was a pleasant change to be in a light scout again.

As I spiralled down at Saint André, I saw that the aerodrome was crowded with machines. A Camel that landed just in front of me was turned over on her back by the high wind, so I put my machine down very carefully. A senior officer who happened to be watching was good enough to say that this was the neatest landing he had seen that day, so I asked him to give me a D.H.4 that I might proceed to my squadron. Unfortunately, Sergeant Piercy was in the act of taking off in the only machine allotted to 55 and passed over us as we talked.

I spent the next two days waiting for despatches for the 8th Brigade. The crowded state of the aerodrome was due to the fact that many nearer the Line had been abandoned, and also to the presence of numerous brightly painted Camels, which had been rushed over from the night defence squadrons of London to do ground strafing.

As I passed west of Amiens, I could see but few indications of the great battle beyond the fact that a number of our aeroplanes were standing in open fields.

No one knew to what extent the French had been driven back, but it was believed that they still held Paris, as the capture of that city had not been announced on the German wireless; so I flew straight there, as I had orders on no account to cross the Line with my papers.

On coming out of a rainstorm, I suddenly caught sight of this immense place lying before me. It was wonderful to realise that at one glance I could see the home of more than 2 million people. London was always more mysterious, shrouded in fog or half hidden by smoke. Here I could see everything through the clear, moisture-laden atmosphere. Somehow the place had an expectant look, gazing eastwards along the white roads, towards the fighting, and the advancing foe. High clouds above supported, as it were, by pillar-like rainstorms, whose graceful skirts swept the bright green fields below.

All was going well, yet I was not at my ease, for I had already used up one tank of petrol and there was a stiff head wind; I kept straight on, however.

There were now occasional glimpses of light-blue sky above; the weather was improving. At length I began to recognise the country below, Bar-le-Duc, Ligny, then Toul and Pont St Vincent; presently Mount Zion itself hove in sight, looking more friendly in its vivid spring green than the low, black coast of England, which had faded away behind my Bristol three days before.

As I landed, I saw the General and C.O. walking up the aerodrome, so took my precious despatches from under my cushion and handed them to the former.

'I heard you had started, so I came over,' he said; how glad I was that I had come straight through.

'Four mags. Willie?' asked Gray; fortunately for me, there were.

Everyone was much concerned about the fighting up north; we were already partially cut off by the advance of the enemy, and it was felt that we ought to be back on the British Front in the hour of peril.

Raids had been carried out on Kaiserslautern and Mannheim during my absence. Thakrah and Fluke had been taken prisoner as had also Sergeant Hodge, who had been flying with an American.

This latter gentleman had announced that he came from the Wild and Woolly West, and hinted very broadly that he was a handy man with a six-shooter; he was much subdued, however, after his first experience over the Line. It seems that he simply could not stand the idea of being shot at without replying, so that when the Huns began to follow the formation, he turned round to fire at them.

Realising that they had to do with a novice, the E.A. obliged him to land without shooting him; he was last seen going down in a tight spiral, which presumably prevented Hodge from firing; no doubt he 'shot a good line' when he got back home to 'God's own country'.

In contrast, the squadron had also suffered the loss of a very gallant observer in the death of Sergeant Ryan. On the return journey from Mannheim, Sansom had been left behind and attacked by five E.A. during the running fight which followed, Ryan was wounded in the leg, he sat down and continued to fire; shortly after this he was hit in the right wrist by an explosive bullet, he continued to fire with his left hand, until he became unconscious.

Sansom flew home with both inner bay flying wires shot away, his aileron controls were also gone; the machine was so badly shot about in fact, that she was a 'write-off'.

No. 6 was in good health, although Bridgland had taken her to Mannheim, where young Stewart had shot down his first Hun from her back seat. There was, however, a slight crack in her undercarriage, so I had it changed for one of the more fashionable high type, thus bringing her right up to date.

It was like getting home again to climb into the high cockpit. There was little for me to do, for everything was in perfect order, but I liked to sit there and study my maps, or perhaps polish something, or simply gaze forward past the prop, thinking over all we had done together and planning things we might yet do.

The next show was to go to the German G.H.Q. at Spa, to bomb the All Highest if he happened to be there. Fox was leading, while I was given the second raid. Bad weather delayed the start for several days.

We had been so hard at work in March that I had had little opportunity of considering the morale of the squadron as a whole. I knew, of course, that some of the new pilots thought that the raids should be slowed down, so that they could keep up; while the older members of the squadron seemed to think that if people were such fools as to be incapable of getting the best out of their machines, they jolly well deserved to be shot down.

There had always been, it seemed, a process of natural selection, or rather survival of the fittest, but now even some of the old hands were beginning to doubt if long shows could still be carried out in face of the rapidly increasing opposition of the enemy.

Thinking things over in my own mind, it appeared to me that there was no reason why we should restrict ourselves to short trips, provided that the greatest advantage was taken of the magnificent performance of the de Havilland 4.

'High, fast and far' would be my motto, if I were given a flight; but no one would be left behind, a few practice formations at 16,000 feet would cure the slow pilot. Farrington had just been given the D.S.O. for his long shows, what would be the use of Metz and Thionville to me?

Unfortunately, I took no steps to convert my companions to this way of thinking, being rather shy of expressing; worse than this, I listened to all sorts of alarmist chatter, which began to prey more and more on my mind.

On 5 April the weather cleared sufficiently for us to start for Spa. Bradly was on leave, so I took Mason-Springay with me. Finding that our objective was covered by clouds, Fox turned back and bombed the railway junction at Luxembourg, with excellent results.

When crossing the Briey area on our return journey, we came under intense and accurate A.A. fire; I found this less trying now that I was leading the second raid as most of the shells burst behind me.

Seeing that there were no Huns about, I took my raid over some thick banks of cloud, which immediately sheltered us from Archy. Presently I saw Fresnes-en-Woëvre through a gap; then I had to fly entirely by compass.

Meanwhile Fox was still being shelled over the open, but presently he too began to reach the clouds.

It was a grand sight, our twelve machines high up in the brilliant sunshine, with nothing but oceans of white, blanket-like cloud below and pale-blue sky above, except away to the northeast where the ground could just be seen, murky and dark.

Fox was losing height, and presently he disappeared down through the clouds; some of his raid then joined me, and we flew on to a little gap, which I knew, from the time that had elapsed since passing Fresnes, to be roughly over Gondrecourt, well on our side ...

It was an awe-inspiring moment as we sank below those great, racing cloud hills; the gap was small, and I was afraid that some of our people would lose sight of me as it was so dark down out of the sunshine, but Springay kept up a fusillade of red lights and everyone succeeded in following us.

On looking down, I was pleased to see a canal enter a tunnel on my left, and a little town on my right, which could only be Gondrecourt.

As I flew home with the majority of the first as well as the second raid, I was rather surprised to find that several pilots insisted on maintaining very close formation. I afterwards learned that, on seeing my red lights, these gentlemen thought that we were about to be attacked by E.A. not having the slightest idea where we were. They must have been delighted to find themselves safely in the mess a quarter of an hour later!

Fox rang up to say that he had had a forced landing, but O'Lief was missing. I knew that everyone had come 10 miles our side of the Line, so expected that he would turn up. We heard later, however, that he had managed to cross the Line on his own and present the enemy with a valuable machine and a fairly efficient observer.

Wet weather again prevented all work for several days. Life in our wood was becoming more congenial, in spite of the damp. The weather was mild, and all the fresh young leaves were shooting, turning our unpretentious camp into a rustic bower.

I had made friends with Stewart, and we spent many happy hours together, stalking wild boars, which we never succeeded in sighting, firing our revolvers at a target in the wood, or flying round the country in *No. 6*.

One day we were having a look at the monastery on Mount Zion. I was circling around it, looking down my wing into the courtyard below, when I happened to glance back at Stewart, who was taking careful aim at the weather cock on the top of the chapel spire with his Lewis gun. I immediately flew away, for I knew he was quite capable of pulling the trigger.

There were white clouds from 6 to 14,000 feet, with large gaps between, for the day had cleared, though it was now too late for a show to start. We played amongst the clouds for half an hour or so. A particularly eerie sensation was that of stalling down into the clammy folds after landing on top of a cloud.

During these flights, I also taught Stewart to fly the machine from the back seat. It was grand to be up with this fearless young Canadian, and to lose, for the time, all fear myself. If only he could have been my observer ...

One day Gray took up a formation consisting of Fox, Collett, Van der Riet, Walmsley and myself. We each took a new pilot in the back seat, for the purpose of instruction in formation flying. Gray soon tired of this, and dived on the nearest French aerodrome, which he crossed at a height of about 20 feet, with his unfortunate deputy leader skimming the grass below him.

After several of these visits, we returned to our own aerodrome in very close formation. This was not exactly the kind of practice needed by our new pilots, who were merely ignorant of the use of the extra air lever, or 'altitude corrector' as it was called.

On 11 April, the weather was fine enough for reconnaissances to be attempted. Matthews was given a new 375, while I set out in *No. 6* with Bradly.

Very soon after crossing the Line we were flying above heavy banks of cloud; I could see Matthews away on my left. Beyond Metz we found holes through which Bradly was able to take some of his photographs, but this took us a very long time because we had to wait until the holes fitted over our objectives.

I was tempted to go down through the clouds; but reflected that they were not more than 1,000 feet from the ground, and that on our return journey we should have to cross a wide belt of blue sky before reaching the Line.

We managed at last to get all our photos, and returned well pleased with our success. The next day we went on the longest reconnaissance so far undertaken, to Rastatt and Karlsruhe, on the 375 that Matthews had flown the day before.

As we approached the northern Vosges I caught sight of a little scarlet machine travelling very swiftly at our height; thoughts of the 'Wicked Baron' immediately flashed through my mind, for we had heard rumours of his coming south. I kept straight on; the scout, which had been flying towards us, now turned away and flew southeast at a great speed, losing height rapidly.

I reflected for a moment as to whether it was my duty to go after the E.A. or to go on with the reconnaissance but decided in favour of the latter course, as I had no time to lose if I was to take all the photos.

A few miles across the Line, my oxygen apparatus failed. We flew to Zabern and took photographs at 21,000 feet, in perfect weather; then we flew to Bouxwiller and Haguenau, where the aerodrome was fairly busy. Crossing the Forest, we arrived at Walburg Junction, and soon on to Salz.

We now crossed the river, obtaining a glorious view of Karlsruhe, as it lay there, shapely, clean and glittering in the sun. From the air, it is by far the loveliest city of the Rhine. Turning to black, industrious little Rastatt, we exposed more plates, and admired the endless woodlands of the Black Forest on our left.

We were now becoming somewhat exhausted by the lack of oxygen, yet I could not go lower, on account of several E.A. that were attempting to reach us.

Re-crossing the river, we came upon a tiresome railway reconnaissance, Roppenheim, Bischwiller, Brumath and Hochfelden. Bradly then signalled that something had gone wrong with his camera, and pointed northwards, so we went back to Bouxwiller and took more photos.

Having completed the work, I crossed the Vosges, and flew home by way of the Lakes, as I had seen our friends the scouts climbing at a great height south of Zabern, evidently with the intention of cutting us off, should we return by the shortest route.

The fact that I thought nothing of going 30 miles round shows what complete faith we had in our engines.

I did not feel at all well when I landed, so Stewart got a cylinder of oxygen for us to breathe, which drove away my headache for the time being.

Bradly had been so badly frostbitten that he had missed a number of important photographs, and had seen practically nothing.

Meanwhile Van der Riet and Carrol, his observer, had been out on the Saarburg reconnaissance on a new 375. They had met four E.A. and had had to run for it; fortunately their speed saved them.

It was obvious that Bradly would not be able to fly again for some time, and as he always got frostbite on photography, I must have a new observer; Mason-Springay was therefore posted to *No. 6*, and the next day I took him up to practice taking photos on our side of the Charmes.

I am afraid I did not give this gallant officer a very hearty welcome, as my admiration for Stewart prevented me from appreciating his good qualities.

The weather was unfit for shows during the next few days but our time was occupied with practice formations, experiments in cloud flying, and test flights; while football and motor trips through the surrounding country formed agreeable relaxations.

We had now a cinema in the camp, and Miller, our equipment officer, entertained us almost nightly by singing verses he composed on topical subjects. Perhaps I may here quote his 'confidential report', as it is full of the spirit of the squadron:

He's a fellow of undoubted great ability,
As a pilot he is safe and he is sound,

In the air he flies preserving his stability,
And you never find him stunting near the ground.
His use of D.H.4s is economical,
He rarely does a thing that would be rash,
And it strikes on as a matter almost comical,
To suppose that for a moment he would crash.
He's a specialist in altitude photography,
As a leader of formations he's I-T,
Equipt with a good knowledge of topography,
And we call him, with respect, of course, Fifi.

On my 20th birthday, Gray told me to take over B Flight from Fox, who was going home. I also received another gift in the form of a Croix de Guerre. The French had sent four to the squadron, and they had been allotted to Collett, Ward, Palmer and myself.

Our next job was a reconnaissance to Metz and Sarre-Union, on A Flight's 375. We encountered much cloud both above and below, and were annoyed by E.A. who used them as cover whilst stalking us.

Having failed to get all our photos, we went out again the next day. Flying towards Metz at 19,000, we saw much Archy going up on the other side of the river, and then made out the twelve machines of our raids going north against a strong wind; 'Poor fellows, they are catching it hot, thank heaven I'm not down there!' I thought as I watched the long trail of smoke.

Just then I happened to look straight below me, and there, not a hundred yards away, was a fat enemy two-seater coming in the opposite direction, apparently also engaged in watching the raids, while gaining height in order to go and photograph the French.

I signalled to Springay to fire; but the E.A. put its nose straight down, diving away so fast that I expected to see its wings come off. It was useless to follow.

As our machines passed, we saw several scouts form a procession some distance behind them.

We now arrived over Frescarti aerodrome, and had to begin taking photos. As we circled over Metz, the A.A. people turned their attention to us, but the result was merely of academic interest, Archy could not reach 22,000 feet.

We then flew to Bolchen and Saarbrucken, finding a new aerodrome on the way, and returned home by way of the Lakes.

On 2 May General de Castelnau, who was then in command of the southern group of French armies, inspected the squadron and presented our Croix de Guerre on parade. Stewart very nearly spoilt the effect by taking photographs with a contraband camera at the critical moment, but fortunately he was not detected.

The next day the raids went to Thionville, while we carried out a reconnaissance. It was now my turn to lead the first raid, the objective given being Thionville once more; we started on the next day during a short fine interval. Black clouds were already rolling up as we left the ground. We met Jones leading the second raid, at 14,000 feet; it was an impressive sight to see our twelve machines against the background of storm, and it made me realise my new responsibility.

We went to the Line but could see sheets of rain falling to the westward, and I knew that if I went on, it would be impossible to keep the show together; we should merely run the risk of more people getting lost and landing on the wrong side. I therefore returned to the aerodrome, much disappointed at the failure of my first effort.

Gray accepted my decision without a murmur; he even said he was sorry that we had been sent off in such vile weather. This made me even more determined to succeed at all costs on the first opportunity. The next few days, however, were quite impossible for raids.

Not being satisfied that our formations were sufficiently compact, I took out a number of practice flights, often in very bad weather. On these occasions Stewart accompanied me whenever his own pilot was not flying. He was always worrying me to take him across on dud days to shoot up enemy aerodromes *a la* Bishop, but the gods would not consent to this, much to my secret relief.

One evening Metior sent up a number of his balloons, each carrying a light. We fired at these with machine guns, which had been placed round the aerodrome as A.A. defences. It was great fun watching the bright tracers, but it was fortunate that there were no casualties in Xirocourt, for a number of shots went swinging low down over the hill in a distinctly ominous manner.

When the shooting was over, we dressed Roger in Carrol's pyjamas and put him in the latter's bed. On coming in Carrol, for some reason best known to himself, concluded that Sticky had done this thing; he therefore emptied the contents of a fire bucket over him. Roger ran into the mess, trailing his costume, while Carrol fled into the wood. When we had all gone to bed he returned, climbed onto the roof of our hut, and poured water down the chimneys, causing clouds of steam to rush from the stoves. He was then squirted with fire extinguishers.

Palmer and Wild bought a toy steam engine, with which they played in their room on wet days. One of them made a small windmill, which they worked by means of a string from the fly wheel; we were all called in to feel the draught that this was supposed to make, but were quite unable to detect it.

On 15 May we again set out for Thionville, with Walmsley leading the second raid. No sooner had I left the ground than my radiator began to steam, but as my oil pressure was satisfactory, I increased my speed to 80mph so that the extra draught would cool my engine.

Even so, I was obliged to throttle down several times, and it took me an hour and a half to reach 12,000 feet. I was not going back without reaching the objective this time, so crossed at Thiaucourt without further delay.

We naturally came in for some very accurate A.A. fire, from which Walmsley, who was high above, seemed fairly immune. I now flew almost level at full speed, turning slightly every few seconds; my engine began to get cooler, and we actually arrived at our destination at 14,000 feet.

Not wishing to kill any of the inhabitants of Thionville, I released my bombs as soon as I reached the railway sidings; unfortunately, most of my followers immediately did the same, instead of waiting a few seconds, as ordered; the result was that most of the bombs fell short.

As I looked down the river towards Trier, everything looked open and inviting; why had we not been sent further afield? If the squadron was to be restricted to raids on places like Metz and Thionville, I was indeed too late, but I felt convinced that long shows were still possible, provided that we made the best use of our machines.

We turned and flew homewards, keeping well east of the river, so as to avoid Metz.

This show was not an inspiring debut for a new leader, a fact that was not hidden from the old hands at the time. Walmsley declared that I forgot that I was supposed to be leading the raids, and carried out reconnaissance of the Boulay-Morhange area on the way home. The squadron had always taken the shortest route, regardless of Huns and Archy.

A de Havilland '4' in France, 1918.

Airco DH.4 from the rear, just after take-off, c.1918. (DeGolyer Library, Southern Methodist University via WikimediaCommons)

The four recipients of the Croix de Guerre. The man on the right is Williams, hands visible by his sides. The others are Ward, Collet and Palmer. The person who presented the Croix was General de Castelnau. (RAF Museum, Hendon)

A pilot and his gunner about to take off. Captain Williams would have taken this photograph. (RAF Museum, Hendon)

The squadron mechanics. Captain Williams commented how highly he thought of these men; the mechanics were crucial to the success of the squadron, keeping the planes in the air. (RAF Museum, Hendon)

55 Squadron during their final year of the war, at Tantonville, near Nancy. (RAF Museum, Hendon)

General de Castelnau presenting the Croix de Guerre medals on the airfield itself. Williams is the nearest person to the camera. A DH4 is visible in the background.

The family trunk containing Captain Williams' memoir

A glimpse inside Uncle's mysterious trunk.

The Inscription on Captain Williams' tomb.

7

COLOGNE

Lovely weather had now set in; I stood on the road alone watching the soft light on the woods and the purple of the far-off mountains; the earth was wonderfully beautiful – '*Ach wie hässlich bitter ist das Sterben!*' (i.e. 'O, how bitter a thing it is to die!') – but the thought was not so terrifying as it had been a year before.

I stood there until the light faded into greyness and a chilly wind began to rise as night came on; then I went to see Gray and told him the opinion I had formed with regard to the possibility of long shows.

The next day, when Springay and I returned from a reconnaissance, we heard that Collet's raids had been attacked by a large number of E.A. at Saarbrucken, and that Sansom had been shot down in flames. Several other machines had been badly shot about.

Parke, a young Canadian observer, was wounded in the right leg; he sat down and bandaged himself as well as he could, then, being unable to use his gun any longer, he took a complete set of photographs of the objective.

I was deeply grieved by the loss of Sansom, who was one of the bravest men I ever had the honour to meet.

The night-bombing people at Ochey were sorry to hear that the days of our usefulness were numbered, and many of our own people were inclined to share the same view. Meanwhile it had been discovered that *No. 6* had been suffering from air leaks, which caused the overheating of which I had complained.

The morale of the squadron was somewhat restored by a highly successful raid on Metz the following day, led by the imperturbable Farrington, whose bombing proved extremely accurate.

Springay and I had just landed from our reconnaissance, and heard the good news of the safe return of the raids, when I met the C.O.

'Guess where you're for tomorrow, Willie,' he said.

'Trier?'

'No a damn sight further than that.' I guessed the truth, but modesty forbade me to say so.

'Coblenz?'

'No, no, somewhere you've never been before.'

'Cologne?'

'Yes, you're off to Cologne with six machines; we can't send twelve, you'd have to take every bus that's serviceable, you'd be held back by the slow ones, and the petrol consumption is too high on some for them to do the trip.'

We discussed details together for a few minutes in front of the hangars. As soon as I was alone, I was pounced upon by Stewart and the others, who demanded to be instantly informed as to where we were going. When they heard, they all demanded places on the show, so that the only way to decide was to draw lots.

Some, mindful of the grilling they had received on the previous day, obviously thought that none of us would reach Cologne; not a few there were who must have heard the news with dismay; yet the squadron volunteered to a man.

Farrington, Collett, Colqhoun and I met in Gray's little office; having decided which were the best machines to take, the C.O. called in the flying officers to draw lots. This was done in deep silence; I watched each face in turn, to some came a far away, yet determined look, to others one of disgust and disappointment.

Van der Riet caught me as soon as we left the office.

'Look here Willie, I must go, I'm in your flight, and my bus is going,' he said earnestly.

'No Van, they'll want you to take on the flight after tomorrow,' I answered, although I did not really think this.

'Oh rubbish!' he exclaimed.

Bridgland, Pace and others were equally emphatic in their protests, while both Farrington and Collett offered to lead the show should I feel that my experience was unequal to the task.

Meanwhile Gray had taken up *No. 6* in order to satisfy himself that there was no longer any overheating; I walked up to the aerodrome just as he landed in the growing darkness; it was very reassuring to have his opinion that everything was in order. We then went round to see that all the necessary preparations were going forward. It was 10 p.m. before our hard-working mechanics left off that night.

Presently I went to have a look at my maps in my room. I no longer used the large scale maps issued to pilots and observers, except for reconnaissance purposes, as I had bought some of a much more convenient size in London when on leave.

Gray came in and gave me a chart showing the various objectives that could be reached in different winds; while Walmsley implored me to take another machine, as it would ruin my chances if *No. 6* began to overheat. I was unable to accept this advice: it would be half the battle to be in my own office. It did not occur to me that several of my followers would be in machines that they had never flown before.

I wrote a letter, which was intended to comfort my people in the event of my being killed, and went to bed.

Next morning I woke early, and people were already moving about – 'Cologne!' I thought, shivered and jumped out of bed. Metior promised favourable weather, with very little wind; the objective would most probably be clear, though there might be a few clouds part way.

We all had breakfast; the machines were taken out and run up, then they were taxied to their starting positions and filled to the brim with petrol.

As I sat in my office, feeling just a little overcome by the weight of my responsibilities, Berry, the padre, climbed up to shake hands and wish me luck.

We started up our engines, as Gray, Collett and Farrington took off in the squadron's three 375s, in order to escort us as far as Metz.

I soon followed with my raid and two spare machines. We went away south, climbing rapidly. Everyone tried hard to keep up with *No. 6*; at one time Bell fell rather far below us, whereupon the ever watchful Springay lent over the side and beckoned to him to come up into his place. Walmsley, who saw this incident, was hugely delighted.

At 5,000 feet I swung north again; our escort seemed to hang motionless above us, high up on our left, their noses in the air.

We crossed the Line half an hour after the start, 12,000 feet above Nomeny. For some little time I had been watching two scouts flying at a great height ahead of us.

'This is a fine thing, Huns already.' I thought to myself; however, I now made them out to be Nieuports of a very recent type. Collett thought otherwise – 'Rat, tat, tat, tat, tat!' went his front gun; the Allied airman thus favoured immediately took refuge in the middle of my formation, while his companion fled.

Presently Archy began to burst amongst us, and the Nieuport went down in a log dive for his own side.

The visibility was good, there appeared to be little or no wind, and I was able to steer an exact course. The well-known reconnaissance area, over which we were now passing, looked almost friendly. Whitelock, one of our spare machines, turned homeward on seeing that he was not wanted; but Keep was lagging behind so Jones flew on with us, hoping to take his place.

We were now at 14,000 feet and, I thought, safely past the Scylla and Charybdis of Metz and Saarbrucken. Presently the 375s left us, followed most reluctantly by Jones, for Keep insisted on following us, although far below. We should have arranged a signal by means of which the spare machines could have been informed as to when they might turn back; I should most certainly have taken Jones with us.

We should also have arranged that the spare machines should drop their bombs on some convenient railway and return with the escort if not required. As it happened,

Whitelock got back safely, but he might just as easily have been shot down.

The course I was following lay well to the east of Thionville and Trier, for I was anxious to avoid any E.A. that might have been sent up to defend these places when our crossing was signalled. We could see the smoke of the barrage over each town as we passed: hateful brown patches in the distance, high up in the blue sky.

Steering by compass over the wild and wooded Eifel, I turned a few degrees westward and crossed the Moselle, for I did not wish to meet the defenders of Coblenz.

As Metior had foretold, the weather was now none too clear, while great cloud mountains appeared ahead. Presently we were passing between snowy peaks. I redoubled my watchfulness, expecting to see the scouts come racing from behind the cloud towers.

Keep was still following us; I decided not to slow down for him, as this would have endangered the whole raid; besides I hoped that he would turn back before we met the enemy. Otherwise all was going well.

When we again saw the ground, I was pleased to see a curious circular lake, set in the hills, which was right on my course. We were now at 15,500 feet.

Suddenly the Rhine came into view from under the clouds on our right front; at the same moment I caught sight of a flight of E.A. away to the east, flying north at 16,000 feet. Presently we saw a large town, which might at first sight have been Cologne, away to the northeast. This place had only one bridge over the river, and so was obviously Bonn.

The scouts now flew almost parallel to us on the other side of the river. Owing to the instant danger of attack,

I was unable to admire the City of Cologne, which soon lay before us. The main railway station and sidings ran in a northwest direction from the great Hohenzollern bridge, the main artery of supply to the German Armies on the Western Front.

I did not think that the scouts would attack us over the town, on account of their own barrage; I therefore flew straight towards the main station, intending to bomb along the railway, thus doing maximum damage to the enemy's vital communications. Besides this, the E.A. were still east of us, and in turning northwest along the railway, and then through west and southwest to south as soon as we had dropped our bombs, I counted on increasing the distance from the enemy.

Unfortunately for the success of my plans, the good people of Cologne, and several of the scouts themselves, they attacked us as soon as we reached the city. The result was that when Springay fired my white light as a warning that we were about to reach our objective, most of the pilots, hard pressed by E.A., immediately pulled off their bombs on the middle of the town.

I suddenly found myself over the river and turned quickly, fearing that some of our bombs might fall into the water, as at Trier. I then released my own 'hundred and twelves' on the railway.

All our machines, except Keep, were in very close formation; I could see our observers standing at their raised gun mountings, firing at the scouts, whose noses smoked with long streams of tracers from their double guns. The air seemed full of this white smoke from tracer bullets flying in all directions. I kept on a slow turn from west to south; we had bombed at 15,000, and we were now at 16,000.

Suddenly one of the scouts began to go down, apparently out of control. Keep now flew immediately below the formation. On looking up over my left shoulder, I caught sight of a Hun diving on us; Springay raised his gun and fired a good burst at him; I was about to swerve, when I noticed that the scout had stopped firing, he was falling absolutely vertically past us. We afterwards learned that he crashed near an A.A. battery.

Our speed was beginning to tell, we were gradually drawing away from the enemy. The E.A. that Springay had shot down was a member of a second flight, but their attack soon faded out.

We were now 18,000 feet above sea level, and I was obliged to throttle down, as even Walmsley's 'N' was unable to keep up with *No. 6* at that height; presently he came up and flew very close to me on my high left, which was his place in the formation. I could see him smile as he waved his hand, while Ward stood beaming at his gun, in the observer's cockpit. I could not help feeling that their pleasure might prove a trifle premature.

What little wind there was, was from the east; had it been strong, I should have run before it for the British Line due west of Cologne. It is true that the chief power of the German Air Force lay in that direction, but they would not have been expecting us. As it was, we made straight for Nancy, following the same course we had used on our outward journey.

Shortly before reaching the Moselle, I caught sight of ten E.A. flying north, slightly above our height, to the east of us; I immediately turned a few degrees towards the west.

The enemy could be clearly seen against a high, white cloud, but they may not have seen us; in any case they kept straight on their course. I was glad that I had forbidden the firing of red signal lights when E.A. were sighted; for the long trails of white smoke would most certainly have been seen by the Huns; at the same time, I had such faith in our speed and our observer's fire that I was not anxious.

On the whole, I think the ten scouts must have seen us but simply did not wish to fight. Keep was now far below our formation; I watched the other machines, wondering how badly they were shot about, but I could see the observers standing up and waving to each other now and then, which reassured me.

We now crossed the Moselle, but this time much closer to Trier. The barrage was going up over the town, this may have been seen by a flight of seven scouts, which presently attacked us; however, our terrific speed, great height and accurate observers' fire soon put an end to this new menace.

Meanwhile three E.A. had caught sight of Keep; Patey, his observer, promptly shot one of them down, whereupon the other two flew away.

On and on we pressed; I gazed ahead expecting to catch sight of fresh batches of E.A. for they were flying at a much greater height than usual. We were now above the trackless Eifel, well clear of Thionville; the sky was clear of the enemy.

More scouts were sighted northwest of Saarbrucken, but only long-distance firing took place. We were passing Metz: the Line would soon be in sight.

I resisted the temptation to put my nose down and dive through the last few miles of A.A. fire: we might still encounter the scouts; besides it was not safe to increase the speed, some of the machines might be damaged, and break under the extra strain.

Just as we were reaching the trenches, I saw a number of scouts coming to meet us. As they had circles painted on their wings, I took them to be Frenchmen on their new Nieuports; it was only as they swept by that I saw that each had a small black cross in the centre of their circles. Springay immediately fired a red light, then his Lewis.

A sharp fight followed, but as we were now crossing, the enemy soon turned away.

I had not seen Keep for the last ten minutes and feared that he had been shot down, or forced to land through engine failure; all the others were now on our side.

For once I lost no time in going down to land; yet as I taxied in, I saw Keep's machine outside the hangar.

My mechanics met me with broad smiles on their faces; I beckoned to one to climb up, I felt too tired to shout.

'Is Mr Keep all right?' I asked.

'Yes sir, they're both OK. Been to Cologne sir?'

'Yes.'

My engine was still ticking over when the C.O. came striding up.

'Where have you been, Willie?'

'Cologne, Sir.'

'That's good, all back?'

'All our side.'

Congratulations began to come in, but I felt that they were of little consequence.

Walmsley, Stewart and others told me that they had gone through agonies of apprehension lest I should mistake Bonn for Cologne, while Keep announced that he would have been by that time in Holland had not the enemy forced him to take shelter below our formation, as he never expected to get back with his failing engine.

Sticky's people soon had the photos developed, and our somewhat sceptical authorities were finally convinced that we had reached our objective. Four and a half hours, they had said, was insufficient for the return journey to Cologne.

Sometime after we landed, a flight of D.H.4s came in; they had been as far as Thionville hoping to meet us, and drive off any Huns that might have been attacking us, but unfortunately we had missed each other in the haze.

These flying officers and their leader had flown 30 miles beyond the Line when off duty, simply because they thought we might be in need of assistance.

Cologne was a success for the whole squadron, and the night bombers were the first to admit that they had been mistaken with regard to daylight raids.

8

A CASE OF MISTAKEN IDENTITY

Whit Sunday broke gloriously fine, but the squadron had been given a holiday in honour of the Cologne show.

After a parade service in the men's canteen, Stewart and I went to have a look at Reynold's machine, which lay on a trailer. Wondering peasants in their picturesque Sunday best stood around, while small boys counted the bullet holes. Three months later, I was to inspect my own machine in very similar circumstances, but alone.

Enemy reconnaissance activity had lately been considerable; in fact, a Rumpler photographed our new aerodrome, which was being built at a place called Azelot, almost daily. In doing this work the E.A. had to fly over many French scout squadrons, but the latter appeared to take but little interest in the war. I believe they did very little flying; we never met them in the air, except on the rarest occasions.

The C.O. had been up several times on one of the 375s, which he had had fitted with double Vickers guns, but the

Rumpler always seemed to choose a different hour, or part of the sky.

On Whit Monday, when Farrington and Collett had started with the raids, and Van der Riet had gone on photography, I set off in *No. 6* to watch the Front from the Vosges to Lunéville, while Gray was patrolling between the latter place and Toul. Harris, our gunnery officer, came with me.

We had an excellent view of our people going over; I should not have cared for the job of attacking those compact formations.

We flew up and down the Line for several hours at 18–20,000 feet. At last I caught sight of a machine at our height: a tiny though swiftly growing speck, hurrying to meet us from the northwest; this proved to be the C.O. Otherwise we saw neither friend nor foe, although the weather was perfectly clear.

Orders for Liège went up that evening; we were to try and destroy the railway bridge across the Meuse, and thus cut the main line between Germany and the Western Front. Collett was leading the show, while I had the second raid.

The distance did not worry us, for it was far short of that to Cologne and the weather conditions promised to be ideal, the wind, which had prevented the raids getting further than Landau that day, having died down.

I did not think we should meet with much opposition, except possibly on the homeward journey; Liège would not be protected by the defenders of the Rhineland, yet lay far back from the Western Front.

The possibility of engine failure worried me more than the thought of E.A., so I had my water joints renewed, and felt my propeller again and again for signs of trouble in the reduction gear.

Starting in the misty dawn, we saw the sunrise, a fiery ball above the Vosges. Collett took us due west over Gondrecourt, then up the fog-filled valley to Bar-le-Duc, where we caught sight of the aerodrome half covered with white vapour.

The Forest of Aragon now lay to the north of us, but our leader took us much further west than I had expected, and I was soon quite off my map. The mist hung over the plains beneath us, and although it was quite easy to see the ground, there appeared to be no landmarks of note.

Presently the line came into sight, straggling white trenches that showed few signs of war; I was surprised to see that they curved northward on our left, and shortly afterwards made out the city of Rheims. We were rapidly drifting westward as we flew north.

Several E.A. were now sighted flying at a great height. One of the enemy's crack pilots was known to be working on this part of the Front, so we naturally wondered whether one of these lone machines was his. In any case, no one attempted to interfere with us.

Farrington had once told me that, as the second raid had the disadvantage of being behind the First, it was only fair for the First to be 'in the sun' as much as possible; I had therefore taken up a position on Collett's left. Knowing that we were going too far west, I flew very close to him, trying to edge him away eastward, but without success.

As Collett was leading the show, we had no choice but to follow with ever increasing anxiety.

At length the wooded nature of the country became less marked, while houses became more numerous; then a town, with an important railway junction, came into sight. I knew, of course, that this could not possibly be our objective but decided to bomb the railway, as it was high time we were turning homewards.

Collett flew right over the town, which I took to be Charleroi, without bombing the railways, and carried on in an easterly direction. I decided that if he did not turn homewards within the next quarter of an hour, I should be compelled to leave him through lack of petrol; I reckoned that we were over 100 miles from the Line, and we had little more than an hour's supply left.

Presently, however, we struck the Meuse, and Collett dropped his bombs on railway sheds near the town of Namur; we then turned southward. The rest of the journey was without incident but for the fact that we lost Townsend through engine failure, or petrol shortage.

As soon as we landed, Collett came up to me –

'Why did you drop your bombs before we got to Liège?'

'It was time we turned back; you dropped yours at Namur,' I answered, 'anyhow, they are all on the main line to the Front up north.'

Orders were repeated that evening; I think we were all glad that we were to have another chance to make the show a success for Collett, who had had nothing but bad luck before.

When we were called next morning, it was clear and calm; the last stars were still shining, and the dawn was breaking in a long silver streak over the mountains.

Breakfast, as usual on raid mornings, was not exactly a hearty feast; everyone's nerves were a little on edge, which spoilt our appetites; yet we felt obliged to consume large quantities of bacon and eggs to fortify ourselves against a long flight, and possibly years of malnutrition in a prison camp! The convention that all excitement should be supressed, and that an air of boredom should be maintained, was not conductive to cheerfulness.

As the little groups of flying officers made their way up to the hangars, our old enemy the early morning ground mist began to rise from the valley and cover the aerodrome. Preparations went on, however; the observers' guns crackled in the wood; the heavy machines were wheeled out, their tails carried high on men's shoulders, they rocked a little as they crossed the small ditches at the hangar doors, and their anxious pilots would catch hold of their wing tips to steady them.

The mist grew thicker, and some, with ill-concealed satisfaction, opined that we should not be able to go after all. Collett and I made our final arrangements; we were to meet at Neufchâteau half an hour after the start or, if we missed each other there, above the left bank of the Meuse at Verdun, thirty minutes later.

The mist still hid the end of the aerodrome, and we plunged through it for a few seconds as we left the ground. I now made a wide sweep to my left, intending to watch Collett take off and to keep him in sight, for the air was very hazy and there was, as yet, but little light.

Unfortunately, Whitelock, who was on the outside of the turn, began to lag behind, so that I was obliged to throttle down and wait for him. By the time that I got back to the aerodrome, Collett was already streaming away westward with the first raid.

Our deputy leader, Van der Riet, now fired a green light and went down to land. This made it all the more important for me to keep the rest of my little flock, so fearing that Whitelock might think his machine too slow, I throttled down still more.

Meanwhile I had lost sight of Collett, and when I signalled to Springay to ask if he knew which way he had gone he replied that he had not the slightest idea. This did not worry me, as we had our rendezvous.

Fog still filled the river valleys; here and there the top of a church tower, or a high row of poplars could be seen or smoke rising in a tall column from hidden chimneys below, like dark pillars from a white floor.

The minute hand of my clock kept creeping round; everyone was keeping up very well now, it would soon be time to meet Collett. We flew over Neufchâteau at the appointed time, yet there was no sign of the first raid; thinking they had gone on to Verdun, I made for that place.

Keeping well west of St Michael, to avoid being seen by the enemy, I flew northward, my engine running almost full out. The sun was now lighting up our planes, making them shine as they rose and fell in their places.

'I'll sing thee songs of Araby,

And tales of far Kashmir.'

I wonder if those Hun will see us, and send word that we are bound for Verdun? They jolly well can, if they want to; we shall meet Collett, then we shall be a pretty hard nut to crack I fancy.

There in front lay the dark mass of the Forêt d'Argonne.

'In those twin lakes,

Where wonder wakes,

Thy raptured soul shall rise.'

Hum, no sign of Collett; well it's just over the hour, perhaps he's gone on. I gazed ahead for Archy smoke but could see none.

The air blew keen and strong, the exhaust thundered unnoticed in my ear as I watched the shelled area pass under my wing – 'I wonder if those poor wretches man the trenches right down to the edge of the river ...'

There was a tense moment waiting for Archy to burst;

'Oh, there they are, below and behind; very poor. I don't think we shall get badly shelled, it's too misty.'

Several Huns were in sight, and I again wondered if we were being watched by the man who had destroyed so many of our unfortunate allies but whose name I can no longer remember.

Over Sedan to the Forêt des Ardennes we go; the fog-choked valley of Meuse now winds along between high table lands, but the atmosphere above is much clearer.

The cultivated lands of Belgium are in front, while to the east float little white clouds. In a break in the fog lies Givet.

Our little formation is very compact; Don Waterhouse is very close indeed, he has been in exactly the same position for the past hour. I search the sky in front for signs of Collett or E.A., but can see neither.

Namur is just visible, very far away at the bend of the river to the northwest I look round to Springay, who signals that all is well.

'Yes, that must be Liège ...'

I crossed the river, and then turned southeast straight for the railway bridge. The aerodrome and airship shed were plainly visible north of the town, as were also a few E.A. flying about down low.

My bombs fell a second too late for the bridge but went down on the railway triangle south of the river. The others dropped their eggs on various portions of the railway, and clouds of smoke began to rise from the station, but the main object of our attack remained unscathed, which caused my observer to signal 'wash out!'.

Under the circumstances I think it would have been worthwhile for us to have bombed from a much lower altitude, as our objective was very small from a distance of 3 miles. Of course this would have meant using some of the machines as an escort above the bombers.

Homewards now by compass, for there were no good landmarks. My altimeter registered 17,500. So that we were roughly 19,000 feet above sea level, and I was glad of the oxygen, which I breathed through a cigarette holder on the end of a small rubber tube from the control.

Quite a heavy barrage was going up on our left.

'That little town down there in the woods must be Spa; I wonder if the All Highest is shivering in the cellar of his château yonder.'

Again all was peace, yet we were still 80 miles from the Line. On and on we pressed.

'Little Miss Melody,
Wandering fancy free,
Over the valleys and hills and dales,
Sweet was her voice as the nightingale's,
Never a care had she.'

Hurrah, there is Bastogne; how well I know those roads; no need to watch the compass now we're back on the old recon. area, but we must look out for Huns, we shall meet them now, if at all, they have many 'dromes between here and the Line.'

A little later, Archy starts out of the void again, but we are above the smoke of the iron works, so that the shooting is not very accurate, the shells bursting with great regularity about 50 yards short of our lowest machine.

As we approached Verdun the air below us grew clearer. I was watching some suspicious looking craft, and wondering if they had just been seeing Collett across, when a perfect paroxysm of coughing, followed by one exceedingly loud bang, reminded me that we were not yet out of the wood. An ugly rent appeared in my left-hand bottom plane, some fabric was streaming in the wind.

Overcoming an impulse to dodge sharply, which would have encouraged Archy, I continued to alter my course slightly in a horizontal and vertical direction, every few seconds. The groups of shells that followed were not quite so close, and five minutes later Verdun lay below us.

As soon as we were well on our side, I settled down comfortably in my cockpit and let the machine fly herself; but as the enemy were only just across the gleaming Meuse, I felt obliged to keep a sharp lookout until we had passed St Michael.

On landing we were told that Collett had flown over the aerodrome an hour after the start, since when nothing had been heard of him.

Van der Riet, who had been forced to land on account of engine trouble, had immediately set off in the first machine on which he could lay his hands but had failed to catch us up; he had flown many miles over before finally giving up.

Half an hour passed, the most serious fears were entertained for the first raid; had they all been shot down, or run out of petrol? They could not be in the air much longer, for it was already five hours since the start.

At last, when we had almost given them up, several D.H.4s came sailing home, their engines humming the low, contented throttled-down song of the Rolls.

'I knew you had been to Liège as soon as we sighted the place, the station was on fire,' Collett told me.

All our machines got back to the Line, but some landed at various places through lack of petrol.

That afternoon General Sir Hugh Trenchard came to inspect the aerodrome. When the more formal part of the proceedings was over, the general spoke to the officers of the squadron, giving us encouraging reports as to the effect of our work, and interesting facts on the general situation.

The flight commanders afterwards had the honour of being introduced to the great man. Our various capabilities were then discussed, while we stood by in a condition of painful embarrassment. Fortunately there was the Charleroi-Namur affair to laugh over.

Farrington now took charge of the raids, while Springay and I devoted ourselves to photography. Going out on 27 May on B Flight's 375, we visited Moselle, Saint-Avold, Bolchen and Kreutzwald, at which latter place we missed the powder factory, owing to clouds.

We were much annoyed by an enemy two-seater, which flew with us from place to place, being careful to keep out of range. I could not make up my mind as to the object this machine had in view; was she reporting our position to some new kind of scout, which could reach our height? Was she trying to make up her mind to attack us, and taking fright every time we turned towards her?

We were not surprised to hear on our return that the wind had been too strong for the raids to start with any hope of reaching their objective, so they had wisely remained on the ground.

On the following day we again set off and took many photos, but, just as we were getting to Kreutzwald,

Springay signalled that he had a jam in his camera that he could not rectify.

The next day Farrington had started with the raids when we set off on a third attempt to take the powder factory, and with a long list of fresh places to photograph.

It was not possible to test the front gun before starting, and when I tried to test it in the air, it declined to fire a single shot. We were now at 12,000 feet; Archy was bursting well on our side in the direction of Lunéville, where the enemy photographic machine was over.

Hoping to be able to repair my gun, I began to climb with my engine running full out. I knew that I should not have time to go down and have my Vickers out right on the ground and climb again before the enemy made good his escape.

When we got to 17,000 feet, I made out the big Rumpler well above us; so we made a wide circuit, keeping him in sight and climbing hard. Presently he began to fly towards his own Lines. I had not been able to repair my gun, but Springay was anxious to have a shot with his Lewis, so we hurried after the enemy, keeping well behind his tail planes for we did not wish to be seen.

I was much surprised at the ease with which we overhauled this machine, but came to the conclusion that he must have throttled down well on our side and started his glide home.

As soon as he could bring his gun to bear over the top plane, Springay opened fire, but, after about twenty rounds, his Lewis struck work. The enemy observer immediately jumped up and let off an apparently unlimited supply of ammunition, which passed us in a long white stream of tracer smoke.

I found it perfectly easy to shelter from this gentleman's fire behind the tail of his machine, for the German pilot merely indulged in a series of slow turns, which were not difficult to follow. He had now opened out his engine, however, and was diving for his own side.

It was exasperating to sit there, with the fat Hun not 50 yards away, right in the Aldis sight, and not be able to fire a shot. Meanwhile, the enemy observer had made a number of holes in both my wings, and Springay appeared to be unable to clear his stoppage; so I broke off the very very unsatisfactory engagement.

The Rumpler went straight on down, leaving a long tail of blue engine smoke, while her observer continued to fire with undiminished zeal.

A few minutes later Springay's gun rang out again; so, having regained our height, we went over. We returned with all our pictures a couple of hours later.

On landing we learned that Farrington had again bombed Thionville. On the way back, they had been heavily attacked by E.A.; Wild, the deputy leader of the second raid, had had his right-hand magneto smashed by a bullet, his engine had thereupon lost power, and he had fallen below and behind the formation.

Meanwhile Palmer had trouble with his Lewis; noticing this, one of the E.A. closed in on them and Wild was wounded in the right shoulder by an explosive bullet, which paralysed his arm. The machine began to spin down; Wild unfastened his fingers from the joystick, and managed to regain control with his left hand, 2,000 feet below.

The enemy leader now closed in to finish them off. Palmer's gun was still hopelessly jammed, so in desperation he flung drums of ammunition at the E.A.

By great good fortune, both Spandau guns failed after firing a few shots. Palmer could see the German pilot tugging at his clearing handles, but he was unsuccessful and presently turned away, waving his hand as he went.

None of the other scouts attacked, possibly through lack of ammunition, but it was supposed at the time that their leader had very chivalrously called them off.

Palmer then sat down to help fly the machine, as he knew that Wild was in a fainting condition. Soon after crossing to our side, he saw a scout; in his distressed condition he took this to be a Hun, but it turned out to be a Nieuport.

Wild was just able to land the machine at Ochey, but as soon as he was down, he became unconscious.

Orders for the raids were repeated for the next day. As there was no photography to do, I went out in *No. 6* with Harris in my back seat, hoping to meet our people on their way back and render assistance.

Soon after we passed Nancy we came upon a number of the very latest Nieuports flying up and down on our side of the Line. Knowing that these people were Americans who had offered to meet our raids, I waved to several of them, hoping that they would go with me, but they declined to do so.

We crossed at 17,000 feet, and flew to Metz, which was passed at 18,000 feet. Unfortunately, Harris collapsed into the bottom of his cockpit at this place. He was, as he was never tired of repeating, a C3 man, and I had been foolish to take him but had not liked to ask any of the observers who were having a rest.

It struck me that if I began to throw the machine about in a scrap, 'Guns' might jam the controls with his lifeless or unconscious person, so I flew back to the Line much disappointed.

As there was no sign of life in my back seat when we got down to 5,000 feet, I began to think that Harris really must be dead and wonder if he had been hit by a piece of Archy; however, he recovered slightly before we landed.

A good story appeared in the newspapers about this time: the American pilot who had so needlessly frightened Palmer, had given out that he had rescued our machine from the Huns, and that our pilot had afterwards shaken him warmly by the hand, exclaiming 'Gee, boy, you sure handed out the slick line!' or some such nonsense.

There were some hard things said about 'Those damned Yanks' after this.

9

KARLSRUHE, TRIER
AND COBLENZ

Next morning we set out with twelve machines for Mannheim, Jones leading the second raid. We were all very tired, for we had been up before dawn every morning for a fortnight; I do not think I really woke up until Archy coughed in my ear as we went over at Baccarat, an hour after the start.

The weather was clear, although there was a strong north-easterly wind, which would be helpful on the return journey. I was much puzzled by the movements of the second raid, which, instead of keeping with us, was getting further and further away on our right. It seemed fairly clear that Jones was making for Karlsruhe; possibly one of his Selson pumps was out of action, so that he could not go to Mannheim.

A large white enemy two-seater flew with us at a little distance, and a number of E.A. could be seen climbing to the attack. It was popularly believed that this two-seater, which had often been seen, carried the C.O. and adjutant of the scout squadrons, who wished to observe the conduct of their pilots in the face of the enemy, but it was more probably a wireless reconnaissance machine, detailed to give information as to our course. This was signalled to the scouts by means of large white arrows on the ground.

My own formation was not keeping up well, and I was obliged to reduce my speed several times. Under these circumstances, I decided to go to Karlsruhe with Jones; we were presently crossing the Rhine, and saw the city spread out before us.

After our experience at Cologne, I was anxious not to pass over the town before reaching the railway sidings and munition factories, for I knew that most of our pilots would not keep their bombs for the latter, if there was a scrap. I therefore approached the objective from the southeast.

The scouts were now close upon us, but although there was a good deal of long-range firing, they did not press their attack. Away went our bombs on the railway sidings; while Jones chose the large munition works, on which he made the best shooting I ever saw.

We were just getting clear of the barrage, and I was looking round to admire the results of the second raid's work, when something made me glance up over my left shoulder; a scout was coming down on us out of the sun, in a very steep dive; I swerved violently.

The scout shot past us, Springay tried to fire his double Lewis but failed, the special triggers jamming. Anderson was flying just behind and below us; the E.A. fired into his machine at very close quarters, there was a puff of smoke, and a huge flame burst from the petrol tank of the D.H. sweeping right over the tail.

The fuselage went straight down, while the wings, which had come off, floated over and over like dead leaves.

Springay had now got his guns to go, and was firing at the scout, which was making graceful stalling turns, far below. Meanwhile the other E.A. were making some sort of a show of attacking our rear machines.

We had the wind behind us, and were soon recrossing the Rhine. Presently the enemy two-seater got below and in front of us; I put my nose down and gave him a good burst with both guns, causing him to dive away with all possible speed; this relieved my feelings a little.

The scouts were now joined by another party, coming from the north, who attacked us with great courage and determination. Bridgland's machine was being badly shot about from below. Finding that he could not bring his gun to bear on his attacker, Stewart fired at another scout, which he sent down apparently out of control.

The fighting was extremely fascinating to watch; I did not realise our own danger as I watched the curving lines of tracer smoke but expected every moment to see cross or circles fall. After firing one's own front guns, there is nothing equal to watching one's observer's tracers streaming into an E.A.

Strange as it may seem, there appeared to be no more casualties, although the enemy was able to keep up with us for a long time, on account of the slowness of some of our people, for whom I was obliged to wait.

The scrap was only just over, and we were getting near the Line, when I saw a lone D.H.4. coming to meet us; this machine, of course, carried our C.O. and recording officer; how I wished they had been in time for the fight.

As we flew home, my mind was filled with bitter regrets. Why had I been so damnably foolish as to bomb with my back to the sun? Why had I not detailed two observers to look out for Huns and not bother about the results of the bombing? I had failed to reach Mannheim; I had suffered quite an avoidable casualty.

When we landed, we found that Jones had been labouring under a most extraordinary difficulty; one of his map-boards had been blown out of his cockpit and had jammed his rudder so that it had been almost impossible for him to turn his machine, In spite of this, he had gone on 80 miles over, and carried out the best bombing ever done by the squadron.

When it is remembered that at any moment his machine might have become completely uncontrollable, it is difficult to over-estimate the courage shown by this pilot during his long, drawn-out ordeal.

I felt Anderson's death very keenly, for I had known him at 2 A.D., and knew that he had followed me south. The photos of the bombing were my only consolation.

On 1 June, Farrington set out to bomb Coblenz, while I took the second raid, but we were obliged to turn back at Karthus, near Trier, owing to the strength of the wind. On the way back, De Godet's machine suddenly went straight down for about 3,000 feet, where the wings came off.

Several theories were put forward to account for this accident. Haley was firing at some E.A. who were flying some distance behind our formations, and he may have shot away his own tail bracing wires. De Godet may have been hit by a lucky shot from the enemy, or he may have fainted, and Haley may have pulled the machine out of her dive too violently.

In either case, observers should be taught the danger of shooting their own tails, and using their controls violently.

Having the day off, I went to Charmes to see Wild in hospital, but unfortunately he was too ill to receive visitors.

We were fortunate in having an excellent Canadian hospital on the Charmes–Rambervillers road; here our wounded were looked after with the greatest of skill and kindness.

We certainly did not realise at the time how much we owed to these doctors and nurses, and I am afraid they received scanty recognition. Time after time they saved the lives of people who were sent in in a dying condition, while their convalescent patients were always treated as honoured guests.

Not only did this hospital care for the wounded, for visitors were always welcomed, and the war-weary cheered by pleasant company.

On 3 June we set off for Duren, but soon after crossing at Verdun we saw that the earth north of Luxembourg was entirely obscured by clouds; we therefore bombed the railway junction at the latter place, with very satisfactory results, and returned.

When we got back from this show, we found the squadron packing up for the move to the new aerodrome at Azelot. The ground organisation on this occasion was excellent, and we were given no trouble whatever. Each officer was allotted a certain weight for his kit on the squadron transport, but by the time our batmen had finished packing, most of us exceeded this by about 100 per cent; however, it all went on the good old Leylands.

I had never given Azelot more than a curious glance from the air, and had not taken the trouble to study its boundaries; the result was that I came within an ace of landing in some rough ground adjoining, where I should most certainly have lost my undercarriage. Fortunately pride saved me; I decided to land close to our new hangars, as I thought it was undignified to taxi far.

Our new quarters were pleasantly situated in an orchard near the village, but for the first few days, everyone felt quite homesick. Finding that we had left a few things behind, some of us visited Tantonville that afternoon, but we found that our old home had been visited by 'Dagos', who were working on the aerodrome, and that nothing remained, the very linings having been torn from the huts. The Italians who formed these gangs were commonly understood to be members of their Fifth Army, which had fled from the face of the enemy at Caporetto the previous autumn.

On 4 June Farrington set out once more for Coblenz, while I had the second raid. Crossing at Moncel, near Nancy, we were soon flying over a layer of clouds, which completely hid us from the ground. Great was my disappointment, therefore, when Archy began to burst quite accurately amongst us.

Thinking that the A.A. people must have been ranging by sound, I immediately drew away from the first raid until we were perhaps 300 yards apart; for the next five minutes, shells burst with beautiful regularity in the space between the two formations.

I had a very trying journey, as my pressure went down and I was obliged to use my hand pump the whole time. Under these circumstances I was thankful to see Farrington fire his white light on approaching the railway junction at Konz, south of Trier. It had been generally understood that Trier was not to be bombed, as it was chock full of prisoners of war.

I now fell in behind the first raid and dropped our bombs on and around the junction. I had been too busy trying to get a glimpse of the objective through the clouds, and through my oil-covered bombsight, to watch Farrington; it was, therefore, with considerable surprise that I saw that he was going on to Trier after all.

Owing to the small size of our objective, and the above-mentioned difficulties, to which must be added a strong cross wind, the bombing did more damage to the Moselle vineyards than the railway.

We now followed Farrington through the unpleasantly accurate barrage of Trier; I did not know which way he would turn, and so was unable to meet him when he had done his work. As it happened, he very wisely turned downwind towards Verdun.

The remainder of the journey was uneventful, although we saw some E.A., and Farrington crossed the Line for the last time.

The C.O. now went off to coach some American squadrons, which were shortly expected to begin work, and Collett had gone home, so Farrington was in charge of 55.

Orders for the following day were Coblenz, and I felt particularly anxious to succeed, but we were disappointed, for I found the wind was doing a good 60 at 12,000 feet, when I went up to test the weather.

There was some talk of our going to Metz, but I told Farrington that I would rather wait until the wind moderated and then start for Coblenz. I felt that 55 was too good a squadron for short shows, and that we should be allowed to conserve our energies for raids in the Grand Manner.

Unfortunately, the D.H.9 squadrons set off and dropped their bombs just across the Line; this was accounted unto them for righteousness although we were never supposed to unload in Alsace-Lorraine, except at Metz and Thionville.

99 and 104 Squadrons were full of glee because they had been over when the weather had been too bad for 55, but

Farrington was in hot water. Perhaps it was only natural, therefore, that I went to bed that night absolutely determined to reach Coblenz on the morrow, no matter how hard the wind might blow.

When I was called shortly after 2 a.m. a few pale stars were shining through the upper mists and all was still, but by the time we were ready to start a couple of hours later, a blustering northeast wind had arisen.

Crossing under intense shellfire, we slowly pushed our way northwards. As time slipped by, I became more and more anxious lest we should run out of petrol before we could get back to the Line.

Had the wind been directly against us, we could have counted on having it with us on our return journey, but there was a considerable amount of drift.

At one time I was sorely tempted to bomb Konz, but apart from the fact that this was a very unsatisfactory target, I was loath to add to the long list of failures to reach Coblenz, which had lately been caused by the northeast wind.

I decided that if we ran before the wind for Verdun on leaving the objective, we should at least be able to reach our own side, and pushed on.

At last the meeting place of the rivers came in sight, and a few minutes later we unshipped our cargo on the splendid targets thoughtfully provided by the military authorities at Coblenz.

The barrage did not strike me as being particularly heavy, and there were no E.A. at our height, so that I was surprised, on looking back, to see one of our machines behaving in the oddest manner.

At first I thought that the pilot must have been wounded, and that the observer was trying to fly, but was much relieved when she once more began to get on an even keel. It turned out afterwards that this pilot, who had never been across the Line before, imagined that the barrage was concentrated on his machine, and that the curious movements I had seen were his idea of fooling the gunners!

We now ran before the wind in a southwest direction for a long time. I was steering entirely by compass, for although the winding Moselle could be still seen far away on our left, the country below was devoid of good landmarks.

Time was passing, yet the forest lands still stretched before us; we were certainly moving, but I began to wonder if the wind had dropped. Even so, I knew that, barring accidents, everyone should have enough petrol to reach the Line at Verdun and, when a hundred odd miles in hostile country, this appeared to be all that the heart could desire.

As it happened, the wind was good enough to help us, and we all reached the blessed shelled area by the Meuse without difficulty. It was fortunate that we were not delayed by E.A. or too-accurate Archy fire.

Now that we were once more on our side, a little question, which half an hour earlier had seemed unworthy of notice, assumed serious proportions: where were we to land?

The French had a number of aerodromes behind Verdun, but many were quite unsuitable for fast machines, and I had no information on the subject. Although we were theoretically at the end of our tether, having been five hours in the air, I decided to make for Ochey.

When we arrived above the last named place, *No. 6* was still going strong, so I flew straight home.

All our people had been busy with their extra air levers, so that everyone got back to Azelot after all.

Meanwhile, the Wing had been working itself up into a great state over our long absence. When he heard that we had been to Coblenz, the Colonel gave it as his considered opinion that Walmsley and I had been celebrating our M.C.s the night before and had not been in a condition to realise the strength of the wind when setting out that morning.

The two rearmost observers of each raid had seen nothing of the results of the bombing, as I had instructed them to do nothing but look out for E.A. This was gall and wormwood to those in authority but was later fully justified on many occasions, as was also my habit of crossing the target in an easterly direction.

This latter precaution made it impossible for E.A. to dive on our tails out of the morning sun as we dropped our bombs. The direction was, of course, varied according to the time of day.

This was a most satisfactory show, from my point of view: we had reached our objective, in spite of the wind, and had suffered no casualty.

The failure of the enemy to attack us must, I think, have been due to previous heavy losses from our observers' fire; the scouts could not have failed to meet us, had they wished to do so, thanks to the guide afforded them by Archy smoke, high up in the clear air.

It would almost seem that different enemy scout squadrons were allotted the task of defending particular places; if we dropped our bombs on their pet munition works, they would attack us, but if it was obvious that we were going on somewhere else, they would take no risks.

It was only necessary to bomb Saarbrucken to ensure some hard fighting, but although one usually saw E.A. in that district, they would not interfere if one was going to Coblenz!

During the next few days, Springay and I went on several reconnaissances, while Walmsley took over the raids, going to Thionville and Konz.

Our new aerodrome proved quite a busy place, as the two D.H.9 Squadrons occupied sheds on either side of 55, and we frequently received visits from French and American machines. I was often asked to show Frenchmen round, if they did not speak English, but I am afraid I did not shine as a guide. My whole mind was devoted to the work of the flight and squadron and was much too tired to think of anything else. I had done more than 200 hours' flying in less than four months.

Some amusement was caused by the Nines' fitters, who were in the habit of removing the cylinder heads of their very unreliable B.H.P. engines after every other flight.

At the same time, we had the greatest respect for their pilots and observers. When on reconnaissance, I often saw flights of Nines floating along at what appeared to be no more than 12,000 feet, and 70 miles an hour, half hidden by the smoke of appallingly accurate A.A. fire, and followed by droves of Huns.

It would seem that these slower machines were much more difficult to protect than the D.H.4, as the scouts shot down very large numbers, many of them falling in flames. Possibly this was due to the fact that a scout attacking a fast machine is obliged to steer a fairly steady target for the observer's fire, whereas it can dodge from side to side under a slower plane.

Whoever was responsible for sending these shockingly under-engined aircraft to France in 1918 was guilty of an act of criminal folly, which threw away the life of many a brave man. Matthews and Welchman both went down in flames while leading flights of Nines after leaving 55.

One day the major came over to see us in a French-built Breguet flown by an American. They came in rather fast, heading straight for one of 99's Bessonneau hangars; we all expected to see a first-class smash, but the Breguet put up her wind brakes and drew up in a very short distance.

Our unfortunate C.O. had to take these people over on their first show. They dropped their bombs on some place a few miles from Verdun.

The Americans were later equipped with 400hp Liberty-engines D.H.4s, but they never carried out a single long raid.

A day or two later I went on a photographic trip in Farrington's old machine, *No. 4*, and was forced to admit to myself that she climbed considerably better than *No. 6*, as we romped over at 20,000 feet in fifty-five minutes. The petrol system was very complicated, there being a perfect maze of pipes; of course, I turned the wrong tap when some 30 miles the other side. The engine spluttered and began to stop, I soon rectified my mistake but went on my way considerably shaken.

When we got home, Farrington told us that Jones had been killed. He had gone out on a reconnaissance and had met an enemy photographic machine above Lunéville. He had, of course, immediately attacked the E.A. but had been shot, his machine falling on our side. The death of this very gallant pilot cast a gloom over the squadron. He had been out for nearly a year and had been on the point of returning to England, having a great number of shows to his credit.

The next day a strong west wind was blowing, but I decided to make for Trier with the raids, as this place was once more on the list. We took rather a long time flying to Verdun, owing to the strength of the wind and the slowness of some of our machines, but once we turned to cross the Line, we got on at a great pace.

The Hun had an observation balloon a few miles east of Verdun, at 8,000 feet; our observers fired at this, making him pull it down in great haste.

Every little water course gleamed in the light of the rising sun, while the usual smoke haze of this busy district was streaming away east before the wind, leaving the air brilliantly clear. Silver water, vivid green earth and pale-blue early morning sky were a lovely sight from 16,000 feet; yet I was filled with that wretched fear, which would never leave me in peace.

Going downwind with a ground speed of roughly 160mph, we offered but a poor target for the gunners. Sweeping over the familiar Longwy-Luxembourg reconnaissance area, we were soon dropping our bombs on the railway sidings at Trier.

As we turned south on leaving the objective, I saw that Van der Riet's second raid was being attacked by a number of scouts, accompanied by the usual white two-seater. In these circumstances it was necessary to allow our people to close up, so I throttled down, at the same time continuing my turn to the right; this brought the second raid up level with us.

Two E.A. were shot down by our observers, one of them being seen to crash in a wood. Unfortunately, Legge left his place in the formation with the idea, it was thought, of using his front gun and was shot down in flames.

Meanwhile, the enemy C.O. and recording officer became so engrossed in taking notes that they got mixed up in the fighting, and had their two-seater shot in the engine. Their propeller stopped in mid-air, and we all hoped that the resultant forced landing took the form of a nasty crash, for they were impertinent fellows.

Like the whale that tried conclusions with the torpedo, the large white two-seater was seen no more; so she was most probably a 'write-off'.

The scouts continued to follow us, firing from a considerable distance, hoping, no doubt, to bag one of our machines with a lucky shot, without suffering further losses themselves. I had instructed our observers to continue firing at long range, however, and they presently managed to drive the enemy away.

These tactics were the reverse of those taught at the Observers' School in England, but we never saw a machine set on fire by tracers that had travelled more than 100 yards or so, it was therefore obviously necessary to keep the scouts at a distance.

It was most satisfactory to see scout after scout forced to turn away by long-range fire, while very few of their bullets struck our machines.

We were, of course, considerably troubled by drift on our way south, but at last we all reached Pont à Mousson safely.

On the whole, we had been fortunate, but I was rather cut up over Legge's death. It appeared that he had always said that he would try and get a Hun with his front gun, and I could not but feel that he had been influenced by my bad example at Zweibrücken.

10

CHARMES AND METZ

A tender was going to Charmes, ostensibly for the purpose of taking our equipment officer to do some sort of comic official business. There were no lack of volunteers to join the party, and soon we were racing along the good white roads through pretty, undulating country.

Having suffered the discomforts of the back of this kind of vehicle for eighteen months, I felt it was only right that I should now share the front seat with Miller and the driver, in spite of Stewart's good humoured threat to heave me out of it.

On the way we were stopped by a couple of officers of the famous Chasseurs Alpins, who asked us for a lift; we invited them to step in behind; we therefore arrived at Charmes in a somewhat crowded condition.

Having graciously accepted the profuse thanks of our Allies, and the complaints of those on whom they had sat, Miller and I set off to the bank with Stewart, being somewhat humiliated on the way by the discovery that I was unable to give the former the French for overdraft.

Leaving our valued E.O. in conversation with the officials, we went on to a bakery at the end of the pleasant little town, where chocolates were sold at a price, in spite of orders to the contrary.

Having secured the chocolates, we rejoined the tender and drove on to the Canadian hospital, where Stewart was naturally very much at home amongst his own people, while I felt shy and awkward, although they did everything to make me welcome.

Presently we were taken to see Wild, Parks and Reynolds, who appeared to be extremely well looked after. A few days before, a fire had broken out in an adjoining tent; this had been quickly extinguished, but our people, in their helpless condition, had had a nasty shock.

I am afraid I did little to cheer them up, for I was at a loss to know what to say; Stewart, on the other hand, was distinctly successful, for this boisterous lad knew how to be both quiet and cheerful when occasion demanded.

Presently we were told that we must not tire the patients; so, having left the chocolates with the sister, we followed a M.O. across to their mess for tea.

This was only one of many occasions on which we accepted these good people's hospitality, which sometimes took the form of a delightful picnic in the forest. Although the odd M.O. sometimes found his way to the squadron on a guest night, and a party of sisters was shown round the aerodrome and afterwards entertained at tea in the mess, I do not think we did all we might have done in return for so much kindness.

The return journey provided a few thrills, for our driver knew how to get the last ounce out of his engine.

Next morning broke with uncertain prospects. The sky was perfectly clear on three sides, but to the north lay an ominous darkness, the exact nature of which it was impossible to ascertain at that early hour.

Soon after leaving the ground with the raids, I saw that the darkness was visible, for it had an edge, a long straight line from east to west, extending as far as the eye could see. As we climbed above this we saw that an endless flat tableland of cloud extended away northward.

At first I was very pleased, there would be no Archy to speak of, and probably no E.A., while it was quite possible that we should find a hole through which to drop our bombs.

On the other hand, I knew that a north wind was blowing, so that the clouds, which now lay to the north of Nancy, would soon cover the aerodrome and might extend right down to the ground. I calculated that we should have time to go as far as Thionville and get back to Luxeuil before the clouds reached that place, so pressed on with all haste.

There was something very exhilarating about racing over that snowy tableland of dazzling cloud, but not a hole could we find. Presently I began to wish that the enemy would send up a barrage to indicate the position of our objective, but even then we could not have bombed without a sight of the ground.

Van der Riet now turned round and flew away south with his second raid, and having, as I believed, passed over Thionville, I presently followed.

The edge of the cloud was creeping down the Vosges; but *No. 6* had her nose down and her engine running full out, so that we were overtaking this slow-moving line at the rate of 2 miles a minute.

The ineptitude of some of our pilots was brought home to me during this flight, for when I increased my speed by only 20 miles an hour or so, they seemed unable to do the same but hung back, behind and above me.

When we again saw the ground below us, the aerodrome at Luxeuil was still some distance south, while the foothills of the Vosges frowned on our left. I now lost no time in losing height.

As some of our people were slow to follow, I asked Springay to fire red lights. This acted like magic, for the newer pilots thought that they were still over Hunland and that they were about to be attacked by E.A., colour being lent to this by the sight of an observation balloon!

We now saw that the clouds did not quite reach the ground, and remembering Gray's remarks after my first visit to Luxeuil. I determined to have a shot at getting home.

The snowy floor and brilliant sunshine of a few minutes before gave place to dark mist and increasing gloom as we flew north. Although there was no fog, we were presently flying at a couple of hundred feet. Even so, a few machines that insisted on keeping rather high in formation were constantly flying through cloud; so, fearing that they might get lost in spite of Springay's lavish use of lights, I went down to 50 feet.

Everyone landed safely, which was just as well, as we still had our load of bombs.

Several days of low cloud followed; yet this was no real rest, for we never knew when the protecting pall would leave us. Although our actual contact with the enemy could only be measured in hours, and not in days as in the case of the Infantry, we were never, or very rarely, free for a whole day, while a battalion often spent a week or more well away from the Line.

Once or twice I tried to write a few notes about our work, for I thought our experience might be useful to our new pilots, but I found that this frightened me so much that I had to give it up; it was better not to think.

At the same time, I never suffered from nerves; I think we had very few cases of this much talked of complaint, for we slept and ate exceedingly well, but we all got very very tired as the summer wore on.

On the morning of Sunday 21 June I looked out from the door of our little white flight commanders' hut and saw that the rolling hills were still merged in leaden sky. A little wind blew freshly in my face, there was the smell of rain in the grass, the camp was not yet astir.

Presently an orderly in his shirt sleeves hurried across to the kitchen, and a thin whisp of smoke rose from the men's quarters on the opposite side of the road. I liked the freshness of the morning and decided to go for a little walk but presently changed my mind, for another couple of hours in bed was most desirable.

The wind blew round my ankles as I walked back, making me glad that I had put on my British Warm before coming out.

By 9.30 a.m. we were all at breakfast; a few were laughing and joking together, but there was a listlessness that might have astonished a visitor.

The morning slipped away with the usual round at the hangars; only once did the weather threaten to clear, a luminous whiteness coming in the sheltering clouds, which lifted a little from the hills. At lunch time, deep gloom and peace had once more descended upon us, so that I thought it safe to go for a walk with a few others.

We had not had much walking lately, so that it made quite a pleasant change to tramp along the road. Presently we came to a long row of Bessonneau beside a French aerodrome; the correct thing to do would have been to call on the C.O., but as there was not a soul to be seen, we merely pulled back the canvass flap, which served as a door, and walked into one of the hangers. Here, reposing on the damp floor, we found a strange assortment of flying machines.

In another Bessonneau, whose musty air declared it rarely open, we actually found a mechanic, a cheery little man in a blue overall, with a broom in his hand, who said that he would be enchanted to show us the pride of the collection, a brand new Salmson. This machine proved to be very interesting owing to the small length of the radial engine, the pilot sat in front of the wings, and had a splendid view forward; unfortunately he would have been unable to see a machine diving on his tail.

When we asked our friend where the rest of the personnel of his squadron were to be found, he merely grinned, and jerked his thumb over his shoulder in the direction of Nancy, but I fancy the man exaggerated.

We then took a most affectionate farewell, wishing each other every good fortune, and walked home to tea.

That evening the padre held a service in the Y.M.C.A., but our devotions were disturbed by a dread portent in the shape of a gleam of sunshine, and the C.O. began to fidget in his place.

As soon as the service was over we rushed down to the aerodrome, and, almost before the mechanics had time to put on their overalls, the machines were out; there was only just time to go to Metz and get back before it got dark.

Personally, I thought this foolish, but orders had to be carried out. A stiff breeze was blowing from the north, the sky was partially clear, but every moment the outlook changed. We were very little concerned about the weather itself; we should be as safe as houses in our de Havillands whether it hailed or merely blew a gale; the whole trouble lay in the fact that sooner or later we should have to return to earth; should we be able to find our way home through the clouds and gathering darkness? The climb was a difficult one, for we were constantly turning to avoid great masses of cloud. At last I was obliged to fly up a kind of funnel, without being able to see either the sky above or the earth below, but on coming to the end of this I emerged into brilliant sunshine.

For a moment we were alone, then one by one the other machines began to appear, though they were lost to sight in the white folds again and again, before finally rising clear.

Catching a glimpse of the ground through a fissure in the clouds, I found that we had gone somewhat further south than I had intended, and realised that the wind was very much stronger than it had been on the ground, so immediately turned north.

No. 6 was still above the others; Clerke and Sweet were hanging on close below, while Blythe, Bell and Dowswell were silhouetted against the white clouds beneath.

Unfortunately, the clouds left a large gap about 12–15 miles wide on the other side of the Line, and I knew that Archy would take full advantage of the slowly moving target we should present as we fought our way across against the wind.

Presently I caught sight of our second raid away on my right; as I looked out, surveying the scene, I suddenly became aware of the thunder of the exhaust in my ear, the pressure of the slip-stress and the tiny fluttering Union Jack, which I carried as a mascot; all fear was lost, for one glorious moment, in a feeling of wild exultation.

Having throttled down a little, so that the others might close up, we crossed under the most accurate A.A. fire I had ever experienced. Many of the reports sounded like field guns going off close at hand, in spite of the roar of the engine, and our machines were struck again and again by fragments of shell. Strips of fabric were streaming from my left-hand lower plane, which began to bulge a little with the pressure of the air that got in through a rent near the leading edge.

I constantly altered my height, and turned slightly, but I did nothing abruptly, as any quick change of direction would have been noticed by the gunners.

After about ten minutes of this, we reached the friendly shelter of the clouds on the other side of the gap and flew along them to a point north of Metz; we then turned downwind to bomb.

The sun was setting and had already left the earth, but we could see the famous railway triangle, round which flashed many A.A. guns. Away went our cargo, and we raced on homewards, streams of fire darting from our observers' guns, as they blazed away at some Huns who were climbing to attack.

It only took us five or six minutes to reach the Line, and not many more to go down and land. The light was very bad, but fortunately there were no accidents.

After dinner several of us visited the hangars, where the fitters were filling tanks and the riggers changing planes and patching holes; those who were wise went early to bed, for the night was horribly fine.

Silly, who had recently returned to the squadron, took the raids to Dunningen the next day, being prevented from going to Mannheim by clouds. That evening orders were repeated but I had the first, and Van der Riet the second raid.

The wind was still strong when we were preparing to start, and several of the senior flying officers thought fit to give me their opinion that we could not reach our objective and get back to the Line. I was furious at this, and told them that I intended to bomb the poisoners of the *Badische Anilin und Soda Fabrik*, but I am afraid I allowed their words to influence me all the same.

Soon after getting into the air, no fewer than three machines turned back, while some of the others lagged so far behind that I was obliged to throttle down again and again. We had been in the air well over an hour before we had sufficient height to cross the Line.

A long struggle against a strong head wind with a poor formation seemed to be in prospect.

'Let's bomb Saarbrucken, and go to Mannheim another day, when there is less wind, and we have got full numbers,' I thought, as we crossed at Avrecourt.

Van and his party were well up on our left. Archy was only moderate, I preferred to watch shells bursting round the second raid, but much more serious was the appearance of a number of E.A. to the north of us.

Ward was in my back seat, Walmsley and Springay being both on leave, so I knew that *No. 6* would be well guarded, but I did not feel happy about some of the others.

By the time we reached Saarbrucken we were followed by a large number of scouts, but they failed to reach us before we had dropped our bombs.

The objective was somewhat obscured by smoke, but we were able to turn homewards well satisfied with the result of our visit, yet knowing that we should have to run for it, like naughty boys who have smashed the greenhouse and see the gardeners coming.

Van der Riet now flew on my right; beyond him were two E.A., while the others followed, exchanging fire with our observers.

To our intense surprise, one of the scouts suddenly turned and flew slap into the middle of the second raid, firing as he came. Sweet's machine immediately began to spin down, a great piece of fabric or three-ply coming off as she fell, while the gallant attacker made good his escape.

This was not a case of diving out of the sun, but of deliberately facing a number of Lewis guns, and an example of splendid courage.

The enemy pilot may have noticed that all our observers in the second raid were suffering from stoppages at the same time, but even so he took a big risk.

Thinking that Van der Riet was unable to defend himself, I immediately turned back and flew between him and the scouts. One of the latter now came and sat beside me at a distance of about 300 yards; fearing that he was about to try the same game, I signalled to Ward to fire at him; this he did in his usual deliberate fashion, whereupon the E.A. lost no time in taking his departure.

Meanwhile, a great deal of long-range firing was going on. Many of the E.A. were now in a good position to attack us, being high above our little formations, but they failed to do so, although they outnumbered us by four to one.

The Huns followed us right back to the Line, they might have followed us back to the aerodrome, for all the opposition there was on our side.

When we landed I found that I had been right in supposing that the second raid observers had nearly all had stoppages, and so had been unable to fire. Under these circumstances, I think very few of us would have returned had we gone on to Mannheim, but Gray pointed out that the wind had not been too strong, at any rate on paper, and I felt that we had failed through lack of determination.

A number of points should have received attention after this show: the fact that three machines had turned back, that a number of others had been terribly slow and that our observers had suffered from far too many stoppages, but I merely reported these matters to the C.O. and let it go at that.

As for the enemy, the heroism of one pilot hardly made up for the cowardice of the others; they certainly missed a chance of bagging several more machines. On the next day, 26 June, Silly went to Karlsruhe with the raids in company with 99 and 104 squadrons. Ward and I set out on one of the 375s, but had to return from 11,000 feet as the engine was overheating; we then went off in the Elephant, or large-winged 375.

We photographed Bolchen, Sarreguemines and other places from 22,000 feet. Unfortunately, Ward got frostbitten. Just as we were crossing the Line on our return journey, I noticed a great bank of cirrus cloud, as high above us as we were from earth; this made me realise the vastness of the chasm through which we flew. A few unexpectedly good guesses on the part of Archy put a stop to these reflections.

On coming in to land, I overshot, a thing that had never happened to me in France before. Much annoyed, I put on the engine and went round again; this time I brought the machine down at 60mph, instead of the usual 70mph, even then the broad wings made it difficult to get on the ground.

When Walmsley returned to find Ward frostbitten, he was quite upset; I think he held me responsible for this misfortune. Fortunately no one had damaged his beloved N.

The combined show had been a great success, so we were to go to Thionville with the Nines the next day.

The C.O. had visions of 55 being turned into a long distance escort squadron, mounted on D.H.4s bristling with machine guns, and fitted with Rolls engines of unheard-of horsepower. It was up to us to convince the authorities that we could do the work.

'Whatever happens, Willie, don't let the Huns bag the Nines.'

11

FRIENDLY CLOUDS

The combined show was postponed until the evening, owing to unfavourable weather, so that I had time to test the machines of my flight that were supposed to be slow; I was, however, unable to detect any serious faults.

After tea, Van and I met the Nines' leaders at the squadron office. It was arranged that we should meet them above Ochey at a given time, and act as rearguard.

The Nines had been in the air for half an hour when we started. It was a difficult climb, owing to banks of cloud, but when the second raid met us above our rendezvous at the appointed time, our friends could be seen approaching from all directions. The thirty-six machines then set off.

A lovely bank of cloud extended nearly all the way from Verdun to our objective, and if I had been leading the way, I should have flown above this, probably quite untroubled by Archy. But the Nines' leader was made of sterner stuff, for he took us straight across the open, with the result that his formations got most horribly shelled, while we, who were high above him, got off almost scot-free.

Van flew level with us, some distance away on our right; while in front and below us, not easily distinguishable against the dark-green earth, flew the four flights of little brown two-seaters, leaving trails of Archy smoke behind them.

We were constantly obliged to alter our course, in order to keep behind the slow-flying Nines, and when we at length reached Thionville, it was necessary for us to fly up and down for some time in order to give them all time to drop their bombs.

At last it was our turn to unload; the objective presented a curious sight, the whole area being pockmarked by hundreds of bomb craters, yet only one small fire had been started, as far as I could see.

Away went our bombs, and we turned homewards. The leading Nines were now well on their way south. It was very misty, and the sun was beginning to set; the air in front seemed to be full of our machines, so we were able to open out again.

Presently, when looking to my right, I saw a large number of machines flying south above the Moselle.

'The Huns; but they won't catch us now,' I thought. Then I noticed that the front few machines were flying in a close formation and appeared to be two-seaters, being larger than those that followed, but it was impossible to see any markings, as they were between me and the setting sun.

Realising that this was a flight of Nines followed by a whole crowd of E.A., I immediately turned and flew back towards them.

As we came racing towards the scrap, we could see the scouts' noses smoking with tracers, while the observers fired back. Suddenly a flame trickled along the side of a Nine, then the petrol tank burst and she fell a blazing wreck, her wings coming off.

'Don't let the Hun bag the Nines, good Lord, he'll bag the lot, if we don't stop him,' I thought. I felt as if the opposing side had scored first in a football match; I was much too excited to be frightened. A moment later we were diving on the scouts, our front guns rattling in fine style.

The enemy left the Nines at once, some of them making their escape far below, while others stalled up to fire at us. As the Nines swept past below us, I began to turn again, in order to follow them home; as I did so, I saw that one of the brightly painted Fokker triplanes was going down completely out of control.

Our observers were all hotly engaged, while a fresh batch of scouts came racing in from our high left-front, one fellow passing only a few yards away; these people attacked us with much determination.

Angry wisps of tracer smoke were flying in all directions; Sergeant Clare, my gunner, was making the most of his opportunity; presently he fired a long burst, and I could see his tracers hitting a scout that was firing at Don Waterhouse; there was an ominous bang as one of my elevator cables was shot through, but the Hun was going down completely out of control.

Sergeant Clare then swung his gun to the other side of our tail, so as to shoot at another scout, but I signalled to him to fire only on our port side, for if he had hit our second elevator cable, we should most certainly have been killed.

Meanwhile the enemy had had no success, while another of his machines was falling, and several others were forced to leave the fight. A few minutes later our observers had beaten off the attack.

Dowswell was missing, but he had not been with us at the beginning of the fight, so I concluded that he had been unable to follow our rapid turn and had gone on home on finding himself alone; but I felt rather anxious about him all the same.

As soon as we were across, I went straight down and landed successfully with my one elevator, hard on the heels of the second raid. Van had taken the three leading flights of Nines back to the Line, not having noticed our sudden turn.

Our five machines were all more or less shot about. Waterhouse was particularly displeased by the discovery of bullet holes through the back of his seat; he must have been leaning out at the moment they struck the machine.

That evening, Gray and I had dinner with 99 Squadron. I unwisely reminded Major Pattinson that I had often had the pleasure of delivering machines to him when he commanded 57 Squadron up north.

'You always brought us the duds, and kept the best for 55,' he said.

Naturally no one was very gay, on account of their loss.

After dinner, a night bomber came over and provided some fireworks; twinkling lights of bursting shells over Nancy, search lights waving here and there, lighting up otherwise invisible patches of cloud, streams of tracers from some excited machine gunners, rising seemingly slowly into the night.

The deep-throated boom of twin engines came nearer and nearer; presently out of the darkness above us flew a dozen tracers, the nearest French search light went out, the machine gunners were silent; how that observer must have chuckled.

'Bang, bang, bang' crashed out the British Archy battery on the hill; we listened for the whine of bombs, but the Hun boomed on.

We visited Harris and his men at our own Lewis gun pits on our way back to bed. They had orders not to fire unless it was obvious that the bomber knew he was over the aerodrome. A number of these heroes were crouching in the bottom of their holes in a state of panic, although there was then no E.A. within 10 miles.

Once or twice during the night I was vaguely aware of the barking of Archy and the drone of twin engines, but it was necessary to sleep.

As Gray had returned, Farrington was going back to England, so we decided to give a little luncheon in his honour, weather permitting, at the Restaurant Stanislaus at Nancy. The clerk of the weather was kind, so at the appointed time we gathered in the private dining room overlooking the famous square.

The whole thing was quite informal, there were no speeches, but we drank Farrington's health, knowing that we would all be the poorer for his going.

Afterwards we strolled round the town until it was time for the train; everyone tried to be cheerful but without great success. When we finally saw Farrington into his compartment, he admitted that he would much rather go back with us to the squadron than return to England.

Nancy was, of course, a very gay place; large numbers of officers and other ranks of different nations thronged the streets, many of them in the company of light ladies, but such pleasures were not for us who were in the forefront of the battle.

New pilots coming out from England during what proved to be the last year of the war were understood to have been through a most comprehensive course of training lasting many months, to have flown an enormous number of hours, and to have passed a great number of tests in all the arts of aerial warfare.

Unfortunately, it was quite a rare thing for one of them to be able to fly correctly in formation, especially at a height. This was due to lack of practice with our old friend the extra air lever.

We should, no doubt, have taken up practice formations, but our duties already required an enormous amount of flying. The squadron was also sadly divided, the old hands keeping apart from the novices, so that it was difficult for the latter to pick up tips from the more experienced pilots. This was simply due to the fact that Englishmen are apt to reserve their friendship for people they know, while looking with suspicion upon newcomers.

As has already been said, a new pilot on finding himself left behind would often jump to the conclusion that his machine was slower than the others and, knowing that stragglers were usually shot down, would return to the aerodrome.

This was all very well for the pilot concerned, but the loss of several machines had a disastrous effect upon the safety and efficiency of the raids. Moreover, one or two pilots were quickly gaining an unenviable reputation because they never crossed the Line but invariably left their places on our side.

Under these circumstances I let it be known that if more than three machines left us, I should return in order to make a fresh start with full numbers.

However, Silly carried out a brilliant attack on Mannheim on 29 June, with eleven out of twelve machines, and I began to think that the trouble was at an end; I was soon to be undeceived.

Orders for the next day were the same, so we set out with Walmsley leading the second raid. No sooner had we reached 14,000 feet than the rot set in, three machines leaving us in quick succession, while a fourth fell out just as we were about to cross. I decided to return to the aerodrome and make a fresh start, but it seemed a pity not to carry out my pet project of bombing Haguenau aerodrome now that we had got so far.

Having dropped our bombs without encountering any opposition beyond the usual phosphorous Archy of the Vosges, we returned.

When we got home, the C.O. was very much upset; we were, he told us, supposed to be escorting the Nines. I pointed out that there was nothing about this in orders, but he would not be comforted and declared that the Nines would certainly be shot down.

I had given instructions for our machines to be filled up, and fresh bombs fitted, so that we might start again without delay. When Gray found this out, he cancelled my orders on the grounds that they would make too much work for the men, and wanted to know who was in command of the squadron!

The major's gloomy forebodings about the Nines proved correct, for they lost no fewer than seven machines on their way back from Landau.

On hearing of this disaster to 99 Squadron, Major Quinelle set out with twelve Nines of 104 Squadron and bombed Landau the same afternoon, returning without loss. He was given the D.F.C. for this fine piece of work.

Coblenz was our next objective, but bad weather prevented Walmsley from getting beyond Trier; so the next morning I set out with Bridgland leading the second raid.

Believing it to be a wise policy to cross the Line at widely separated points, I decided to make for Verdun, which we reached in less than an hour. We had not got far, however, when we saw that the whole country north of Trier lay under an ocean of cloud. At first I was much disappointed but presently saw that there were dark marks ahead, which might prove to be holes, and decided to go on.

The further we went, the less likely success appeared to be; the dark marks were nothing but valleys in the solid floor of cloud; not an inch of the earth was to be seen.

Yet I was fascinated by my compass; we would stick to our course until I knew by the time we had taken that we must be over Coblenz.

There was nothing but the white ocean below and the blue sky above, all filled with dazzling light.

Strange thoughts came into my mind; the earth was no longer there, we were going off into space, we should go on forever and ever … It would not matter if I ran into one of those hard-looking, solid machines, which flew but a few yards away, for they were not really there; they too were ghosts … Fortunately I did not test the correctness of this theory.

We were getting near, and there was still no gap. I thought of going down through the clouds but knew that by so doing I should break up the formations; besides, for all I knew, the clouds might extend right down to the ground.

By my reckoning we could not now be more than a couple of miles from Coblenz, but there was nothing to be seen, and nothing to be gained by going any further.

We had actually begun to turn when Archy began to burst a thousand yards away on our right. We at once headed for the group of little black puffs, which soon began to spring into existence all round us.

There sure enough, right below us was a tiny fissure in the clouds, through which we caught a glimpse of the Rhine, and Ehrenbreitstein, the fortress opposite Coblenz. Away went our bombs, and we were off home with just enough time to do the journey comfortably.

I again headed for Verdun by compass, as I knew that it would be possible to fly above the clouds nearly all the way. We kept a good look out for E.A., although we were hidden from the ground, but nothing came out of the infinite space around to trouble us.

When we at length reached the edge of the clouds, the yellow earth of Verdun was already in sight. A few E.A. were flying up and down, but they were probably looking out for Frenchmen; in any case, they ignored us.

We slipped across the Line, and settled down to enjoy the long run home, well pleased with our good fortune.

A German account of this raid, which was captured a few days later, made amusing reading: 'Owing to low clouds enemy airmen were able to drop their bombs from a very low height, so that the damage was exceptionally severe.' Having unloaded at 16,000 feet, we thought this a merry jest.

We further learned that the ancient fortress of Ehrenbreitstein had been packed with reinforcements on their way to the Front. A number of these men had been killed, while the distressing result on the morale of the survivors was most serious.

Van der Riet was given the D.F.C. and returned to England about this time for a well-earned rest. It was unfortunate for the squadron that he was not given a flight, for he was an ideal leader, but he had been out for many months and was probably quite worn out, although he would never have admitted this.

My turn for leave had again arrived, but Gray asked me not to take it, as I was soon to follow Van to England. This was a great mistake, for I only needed a few days' complete rest and change to set me up again.

On 6 July Silly set out for Duren, but a piece of Archy let the water out of his radiator, so he bombed the railways at Metz and returned. We went for a long photographic trip to Longuyon, Bettembourg and Boulay.

The next-day orders were repeated for Duren, so we set out with Bell leading the second raid, in ideal weather. As we approached Verdun, however, conditions became less favourable; the sky was covered with a layer of high white cloud, while the lower banks, which had sheltered us on the last Coblenz show, again appeared well across the Line.

Silhouetted against the white background, we made an ideal background for the gunners, who took full advantage of their opportunity.

In spite of all I could do, my machine was repeatedly struck by fragments of shell, as were all the others. I continued to turn slightly and alter my height and speed, but we were constantly followed by the hideous chorus of coughs, interrupted every few seconds by a deafening crash.

There was, of course, no choice but to sit tight until we reached the shelter of the friendly cloud banks some 10 miles ahead. I have been told by ex-infantrymen that nothing but the noise of our engines saved us from shell-shock on occasions such as this.

At last we reached the clouds below, and the shooting stopped; I soon realised, however, that it was most unlikely that we should find our far-off objective, for I had been so intent on fooling the gunners that I had not set my course before losing sight of the ground.

There was a small gap about 20 miles ahead, but when we got there, nothing but forest could be seen, and we had to cross another 30 miles before coming to a slightly larger gap, through which we saw a curious crescent-shaped wood, which I did not recognise.

Thinking that Springay might have noticed this wood on his way back from Liège, I asked him by note to place it on the map, but he gave me an answer which could not have been less than 30 miles wide of the mark; this shook my confidence considerably.

Even though we could not see another hole in the clouds ahead, I think I should have gone on but for the fact that our objective was not very far from the Dutch frontier, and we had been warned that it was most undesirable to bomb the railways of that country. Fearing that a mistake on my part might bring Holland into the war on the side of the Central Powers, I presently turned back, and steered a course that was intended to take us to Luxemburg.

When we reached the edge of the clouds, Luxemburg lay before us; we dropped our bombs on the railway junction, and went on home via Pont-à-Mousson.

We were attacked by a number of E.A. when west of Thionville, but they were driven off by our observers' fire.

I was inclined to reproach myself for lack of confidence as we flew home; the fact that we had flown straight to Luxemburg showed that we had been on the correct course for Duren when I had decided to turn back, but Gray welcomed us very kindly on our return, saying that we had done all that was possible under the circumstances.

This made me all the more anxious to succeed at the first opportunity, so I put up a little motto in *No. 6*, 'Do it this trip.'

On returning from reconnaissance on 11 July, I met with the most serious accident which ever befell me whilst flying. This was entirely due to slackness on my part.

The wind was blowing with great force, so I judged my distance so as to land quite close to the hangars, as it was troublesome to have to taxi in a high wind, and I was dead tired. At the last moment, the 375 began to sink rather rapidly, and I saw that I could not reach the aerodrome proper unless I used my engine. Knowing that the machine was only doing this to annoy me, I refused to take any action.

'I'm damned if I'll give you any more throttle; you'll have to jolly well stick where you pitch!'

I made a perfect three-point landing at a very low ground speed, but the next moment my undercarriage was swept off by a little trench and ridge of earth, hidden in the long grass; we were not even shaken, but I felt extremely foolish.

The Colonel was much amused when he heard of this mishap; so when we got back from another reconnaissance the next day, he rang up to ask if I had broken anything; I replied indignantly that I had not and went up to test the 375, which had been fitted with a new undercarriage.

When taxiing in after landing, I ran into a bit of iron framework, which some fool had left about on the aerodrome, and smashed my lower wing tip, but I made everyone swear that they would not tell Baldwin.

Meanwhile Silly had been to Offenburg and Walmsley to Saarburg, with the raids.

12

OBERNDORF AND MANNHEIM

It is difficult to give an adequate idea of the work of the squadron during those trying summer months, for everything ran with such precision that we ourselves were not aware of the tremendous effort exerted.

Day after day our flying officers went out with the raids led by different flight commanders, while it was possible for us to have one day on reconnaissance and one day's rest, or rather test, between each show.

So consistently good, in fact, was the record of our junior members that it led to their merits being taken for granted and insufficiently appreciated. It is true that we had one or two failures, but they were quietly certified to be suffering from this, that and the other, and hurried off to hospital by our very efficient M.O.

Then our ground organisation not only kept machines and engines in first-class condition but was always ready to carry out emergency work in the shortest time.

One day an American landed with a bang on the aerodrome, smashing his undercarriage and lower planes.

My flight sergeant was much amused because the Yanks who came to collect the machine said that it would take them ten days to repair, while he would have had to have it ready for me to test the next day.

Our next effort was a somewhat unsatisfactory evening show, the objective being Offenburg. It was a difficult climb through clouds; I comforted myself that they would give us a certain amount of shelter over the Line, but as often happens in the evening, they all began to melt away as soon as we were ready to cross.

A number of E.A. could be seen climbing to the attack before we crossed the Rhine, and presently the firing began. We were able to bomb the railway works, however, while our observers kept the scouts at a distance. I believe that the idea is now that the observer should do the bombing; if this is so, the scouts will only have to wait until the two-seaters reach their objective in order to shoot them down without loss to themselves.

There was a certain amount of shooting on the way home, but the E.A. were unable to close in on us, and there were no casualties.

The following morning Silly was taking off with the raids when Whitelock failed to clear a D.H.9, which had been left out on the aerodrome. The undercarriage of the D.H.4 was torn off, but she went on flying. One bomb fell but failed to explode owing to the low height; then the second 112 came off this burst, wrecking the D.H.4, and wounding a man who was standing at some considerable distance.

Whitelock was killed and Bryer-Ash badly wounded. No one had thought of ducking on seeing the bombs fall, for we could only think of the chances of the crew, but we realised that we had had a fortunate escape on examining the damage done by fragments.

Silly bombed Thionville; on the way back an observer was killed and a pilot wounded in a running fight.

The next show was led by Walmsley, who bombed Oberndorf and returned without loss.

On returning from a reconnaissance that afternoon, I found that orders had been repeated. Since we had such a wide choice of objectives, I should have preferred a fresh direction, as it seemed only too likely that the Huns, who were supposed to protect the important munition works at Oberndorf, would have been cursed for their failure of that day, and would be waiting for us on the morrow, thirsting for revenge.

When arranging the work for the following day, Gray always called the flight commanders together in his little office. On this occasion, he asked me who should lead the second raid; I suggested Welchman, and this was agreed to.

We then discussed the formation of the raids, 'front seats' being allotted to the best pilots, who were not acting as deputy leaders. These 'front seats' were always considered the safest positions, as they were above the leader on either side, but they could only be given to people who could be trusted to keep close formation all the way, as on them depended the position of those in the 'back seats'.

On leaving the ground next morning, we flew south-west, i.e. straight away from the Line, in order to lessen the chance of our being seen or heard by the enemy before crossing. When we reached 10,000 feet, we turned towards the Line, this being the only change of direction on our side while climbing. This was my routine, whenever the sky was clear, as I knew that the machines climbed best while flying straight and that it was less tiring for the pilots.

We met Welchman at Raon-l'Étape at the appointed time, but he was a long way below us. Crossing the Rhine Valley, we constantly had to throttle down to wait for slow machines.

A large white arrow on the aerodrome at Lahr was turned by invisible hands as we passed over, to show the scouts which way we had gone. This was hardly necessary, the air behind us was full of Archy smoke and a number of E.A. were already following us, although at a considerable distance.

Leaving this pretty place, we swept on over the dark, forbidding mass of the Black Forest. Presently I was glad to see the scouts turn back; probably they had decided that we were not going to bomb any place for which they were responsible, and thought it was not worth risking their lives in defence of Oberndorf.

Soon the forests became less continuous. I was flying by compass and felt a little anxious about my course, but there, sure enough, lay the little manufacturing town on the Neckar.

There was quite a heavy barrage above our objective, but most of it was too low, and we were able to drop our bombs with satisfactory results; no sooner were we clear of the smoke than I caught sight of a formation of twelve E.A. high above us, against a white cloud to the northwest. These gentry came down upon us at a terrific pace.

Welchman had fallen in behind us to drop his bombs, and was, unfortunately, some distance off; I at once began a slow turn to my left, in order to lessen the distance between us. As I glanced round to see that I was not running into the machine next to me, *No. 6* was shaken by a terrific burst of fire; the enemy leader, who had unexpectedly dived on us from the front, now flashed by not 10 yards away.

I was much annoyed at having lost a chance of using my front guns; particularly as the E.A had got in a good burst; I saw at a glance that *No. 6* would require yet another set of right-hand main planes, as the main spars must be shot through. Landing wires were streaming in the wind, but no flying wires were cut.

Meanwhile the scouts were all attacking with great determination; as I looked round again I saw Young's machine burst into flames and Butler, his observer, jump out; the enemy leader was soon following his victim, however.

Sergeant Nash was also in trouble; steam was coming from his radiator and he was losing height, still hotly engaged with two E.A. His observer was killed, and he was taken prisoner.

Welchman was now racing to our assistance, his front gun going, and, finding themselves between two fires, the scouts were glad to dive away below.

Seeing one E.A. very low down, I watched him for a moment and was delighted to see him burst into flames on hitting the ground.

I certainly felt as if I had been caught in a thundershower without my umbrella, but I was not in the least shaken; I felt that I had seen it all happen to puppets.

Much more alarming was the journey home. Keep, my deputy leader, was flying extremely close to me; presently he held up his arm, which was covered with blood. I was much afraid that as he became fainter, he would not be able to see me properly and might cut my tail off with his prop, which was turning but a few feet below.

Two scouts accompanied us all the way to the Rhine, but kept at a distance of about 600 yards. No doubt they were waiting to see if any of us would be forced to land, in which case they would have put in a claim.

Just as the blue line of the Vosges came into sight, another flight of E.A. came in to attack us.

'So we are not to get home after all,' I thought, 'what a nuisance, I shall not see Stewart again.'

Fortunately these people were not at all of the same stamp as the first, and although the firing lasted until we reached the Line, the only casualty was one scout, who was seen to crash quite close to the French.

As we were about to cross, poor Springay, who was ill with jaundice, mistook Bridgland for a scout and began to fire at him; I banked sharply in order to throw him off his aim, and he collapsed into the bottom of his cockpit.

As soon as we had crossed, Keep, who had flown in perfect formation all the way home, left us to go down and land. He got safely into a tiny field by a French hospital, and fainted as soon as he touched the ground. His observer had been killed by a piece of shell.

On the following day Silly bombed Rottweil, near Oberndorf, where he caused an explosion that was plainly heard in Switzerland. Although he encountered large numbers of scouts, they kept at a respectful distance, and he returned safely. I think this proves that the enemy had suffered heavy losses from our observers' fire on the previous day.

The night people had been to Mannheim, but of course they could not tell exactly what damage they had done there, so a photographic reconnaissance was ordered.

Now Mannheim was a good 100 miles from the Line, but I expected to be able to reach an unprecedented height, as we were going on the Elephant 375, so that I was not unduly worried by the thought of E.A.

The raids having started, we made a leisurely departure. The big machine rose somewhat languidly through the clear morning air; the Eagle 8 engine ran smoothly but refused to exert itself to the extent that I could have wished.

At 15,000 feet I began to wonder whether we should have to get to Mannheim and back, owing to the strong south wind. We were not supposed to cross on a solo reconnaissance under 20,000 feet; but I decided not to lose any more time on our side, and turned straight for the Line, which we crossed at 18,000 feet over Badonviller.

We now saw French Archy going up some distance away on our right, and presently made out a tiny hurrying speck flying away from us at 1,000 feet above our height.

For the moment I was undecided as to whether it was our duty to give chase or go on, but as it would obviously be impossible for us to go to Mannheim if we lost any more time, I did not deviate from my course.

A wonderful journey followed, now over masses of billowy cloud, now between grotesque grey castles, and snowy heights, which rose far up into the clear blue sky above, bathed in brilliant frozen sunshine.

Then again, as the white crags were left behind, the earth would appear with its sombre forest, and far away on our right, the Rhine and Karlsruhe gleaming amid its green woods.

Now and then some aerodrome or railway junction would come into sight, and we would take a couple of photographs, while the local A.A. people would fire a few rounds.

Meanwhile I was not exactly free from anxiety, for my machine would not climb to 19,000 feet, a height which could be reached by enemy machines, while our remarkable ground speed only served to emphasise the strength of the wind which we should have to face on our return journey.

I comforted myself with the thought that the Elephant's light wing loading would allow me to out manoeuvre the scouts at a height, and Quinton, my observer, was known to be a good shot.

We now came to a large clear space with Landau in the middle, and Mannheim in the distance, under dark clouds.

The A.A. people were evidently under the impression that a full-dress air raid was on the way, for they put up a heavy barrage over our objective at 15,000 feet, while flocks of E.A. flew about below us, like fish swimming in the water of some clear lake.

We chuckled to think that the poisoners of Ludwigshafen were shivering in their dugouts, expecting at every moment to hear the crash of bombs, but we were only able to take a few of our photographs, on account of the clouds.

Archy now began to burst at our height, and I was afraid that this would point us out to the droves of scouts below. As it would take some time for the wind to clear the clouds away from the town, I decided that it would be safest for us to take a little trip, and return later.

Certainly we were going still further from the Linc, but as we were already 100 miles distant, an extra 10 would make but little difference; moreover I thought the enemy would expect us to be on our way home.

Having peacefully admired Worms and the surrounding country, we turned south again. On reaching Mannheim we found that the clouds had been replaced by others, but we were able to take a few more photos.

Most of the E.A. had evidently gone down to land on finding that there was no raid, but a few sportsmen had gone on climbing, and were now dangerously near our height.

At last I felt that we had done all that was possible, and we turned homewards, while Quinton fired at the scouts below. I do not think these people liked the position, for they stalled every time they pulled up their noses to fire; in any case, they soon turned away.

Presently the brown haze of Archy smoke above the clouds was fading away in the distance. The fantastic beauty of the morning had given place to the fine weather mist of late summer. Each landmark that came into sight now brought a sense of fresh satisfaction, showing that we were making good progress against the wind.

We only sighted one E.A. at our height, a Rumpler near the Line; this machine, which was somewhat above us, flew away east on our approach. We had then been flying for many miles over a large bank of clouds, and I was not sure of our position or of the amount of petrol we had left, so I kept straight on.

On reaching the edge of the clouds, we were glad to see that the trenches were almost below us. I had no sooner throttled down the engine than a terrific report just below our tail made the whole machine quiver. I glanced round half expecting to see that the tail had been blown off, but everything appeared to be in order.

My first impulse was to jam on the engine, but this would have encouraged the gunners by showing them that their range had been correct, so I pretended to ignore them, and their next shots were very wide of the mark.

A few minutes later we knew that we must be out of harm's way, but we always kept a good look out for the Spads and Nieuports when flying near the Line, as we had no wish to become the victims of a regrettable error.

We had not succeeded in getting all our photos owing to the clouds, but the reconnaissance was completed next day by Bill Pace on a more efficient 375.

Our reconnaissance to Worms was the longest ever carried out by a British machine on the Western Front, but a Frenchman photographed Essen in a single-seater Spad, fitted with a camera but no guns, from a height unattainable by any German machine.

As each long summer evening drew to a close, the air became charged with a slight yet definite anxiety –

'I wonder if he will be over tonight.'

As it turned out, the enemy's night bombers proved most unenterprising; they smashed a transport shed, and caused two or three casualties but failed to do any serious damage. On the other hand, our beautiful orchard was ruined by barricades of sand bags round the huts, and a number of people who should have known better were quite terrified.

Some of these worthies made holes in a hillside not far away, much to the annoyance of the local rabbits, and they could be heard leaving the men's camp each night as they made their way to these uncomfortable lairs.

A story, for the accuracy of which I cannot vouch, discloses a still less creditable state of affairs. The Mayor of Azelot, realising that our presence would probably attract the attention of the bombers, had dugouts constructed for the accommodation of the women and children in case of danger. On the first occasion on which the civilians were ordered to take shelter, they found their dugouts already full of persons in khaki!

It was necessary to send for an officer before these heroes could be persuaded to leave. As the bombing was most inaccurate, much the best plan was to stay comfortably in bed.

Another evening amusement was known as 'squirting'. This would not have been funny but for the fact that this unfortunate officer invariably lost his temper and made use of the most picturesque language. This individual, who lived in a hut by himself, was in the habit of going to bed at an early hour. Armed with syphons, we would creep up to his window and open fire with devastating effect.

'Oh stop it you …! I'm not an A1 man! I'm not an A1 man!' he would shout, 'I'll tell the … C.O. about you, I'll tell the … Colonel in the morning, and have you all … well court-martialled for ragging me!'

13

DULCE ET DECORUM EST ...

Stewart came back from leave a day or two later, and, as Bridgland had just left, there was an opportunity for us to fly together.

I had become very tired of late, but my friend's return was like oxygen at 20,000 feet, for he was full of plans, tremendously keen and perfectly confident.

There was talk of a reconnaissance to Friedrichshafen on Lake Constance; of course we should go, and what was more, we should take a couple of 20lb bombs with us to blow up 'the whole outfit, or at least have a blamed good try'.

As it happened, the Italians sent a machine from the other side of the Alps, and orders never came through, much to Stewart's disgust. He told me, however, that I must take him to Essen, or failing that, Cologne.

This was no idle talk of a new hand, he had been with the squadron for five months, during which he had taken part in a great number of shows. Fear simply had no part in him, his whole heart was set on doing great deeds; he would have made a grand scout pilot.

'I shall be killed, Willie, but I shall hit the high spots first!'

Stuttgart was up in orders, but matters were somewhat complicated by the fact that we were to escort the Nines. It was decided that we should start half an hour after the other squadrons, and meet an hour later over Badonviller.

The air was very clear; clouds, Alps, forests, everything was only too plainly visible, except the Nines.

Just as we were approaching the Line, I caught sight of Archy smoke very far away on the other side, and realised that the other squadrons had hurried over before time. This was very tiresome, as they would have brought all the E.A. into the air; on the other hand, an hour and a half was a long time for them to spend on our side if they were to reach Stuttgart.

Soon after entering the usual Vosge Archy, we saw that the Schwartz Wald was completely hidden by a great table-land of cloud at perhaps 10,000 feet over the mountaintops.

This sight was a great relief; we would fly by compass over the clouds and possibly find a gap at Stuttgart. I spent the next few minutes watching the drift through my bomb-sight, for we were fairly free from A.A. fire now that we were over the Rhine valley.

Presently, however, we saw Archy going up to the S.E. and made out the Nines followed by droves of Huns. It was obvious that they were making for Offenburg, and for a moment I was in grave doubt as to what I should do; my orders were to go to Stuttgart; but we were supposed to be escorting the Nines, so we could not leave them to the scouts.

We turned south and raced after the Nines, but they had now dropped their bombs and had turned homewards. We unloaded on the railway sidings as quickly as possible, and followed.

Although it was impossible for us to catch up our friends, the scouts must have seen the Archy smoke high up behind them for they failed, I believe, to bring down any of the Nines, and presently turned their attention to us.

Fortunately the E.A. were rather low, but long-range firing began. As we were crossing the Rhine, two fresh Scouts came diving in on us from our high right. Stewart immediately raised his Lewis and fired a good burst at the foremost, who then put his nose straight down and flashed past us without firing a shot.

As the second scout flew away, Stewart lent over in the most perilous manner and fired another burst after the first; then he waved to me to show that he had got it, and began to dance about in his cockpit.

Presently we met two fresh flights of E.A., who attacked us with great determination. For once I was not sorry to see them come, for I felt sure I should see one or two of them shot down; it was almost a case of 'Ducky, ducky, come and be killed'. It would have been a shame if Stewart had had nothing to fire at all the way home!

It was delightful to watch my observer's tracers striking scout after scout, forcing them to turn away or dive, but I was afraid that White and his second raid, who were flying on my left, and slightly behind, were having a hot time, so I turned in their direction in order to allow them to draw level.

Unfortunately, White turned away every time I turned towards him, so that we were soon flying south-southwest almost parallel to the Line!

I was much too excited to be frightened, but I expected every moment to see disaster overtake one of the other machines; every observer was firing and tracers were flying in all directions. Little puffs of blue smoke kept coming from the exhaust of the machine flying next to me; I half expected to see it burst into flames.

Tracers shot in angry wisps through my wings, yet another new wing would be required for *No. 6* when we got home.

Meanwhile Welchman, White's Deputy Leader, had had his machine badly shot up, and Beasley, his observer, wounded in the leg. This plucky little fellow sat down, and continued to fire as opportunity offered.

We crossed at last without loss. When we got down, our observers claimed several E.A., and to my great delight, Stewart was put in for the Distinguished Flying Cross. During the five months he had been in the squadron, he had been on more than forty long shows, he had destroyed at least three E.A., he had taken innumerable photographs, and his keenness and devotion to duty had been an example to the whole squadron – so wrote the C.O.

The next day we went on a reconnaissance of the Saarbrucken area. It was fine weather, and all went well until Stewart's oxygen failed; he went on with his work until he grew faint, and had to sit down.

As there were no E.A. about, I went down to 15,000 feet, where Stewart was able to carry on.

As we were coming towards the Line on our return journey, we saw a patrol of eight scouts flying in a very close formation, D7 Fokkers. Stewart signalled that he wanted to shoot one or two; he might certainly have had a shot if we had been above the Huns, but under the circumstances I thought it best to use the shelter of a friendly cloud in order to slip across to our side.

Meanwhile Silly, who had set out for Cologne with the raids, had reached Coblenz. Duren was up in orders.

The early morning of 1 August was calm and clear, the weather report was good, the C.O. full of hope.

As we walked down to the aerodrome along the white road past the sleeping village, an engine was being run up, I felt like a Christian martyr on the way to the Colosseum.

An observer was testing his gun; 'Rat-tat-tat-tat!' rang out sharply in the dusk, as the flashing tracers lit up the faces of the men. *No. 6* was already out and the flight sergeant was about to start up the engine for me.

My heart beat a little faster as I got into my heavy Sidcot, for the little voice of fear would never be silent, in spite of all that pride could do – 'You have had a long run, you have had a lot of luck, but that does not mean that you will not get killed in the end.'

At this moment Stewart looked into my little office, he too was anxious.

'You're agoin' to git right there, now ain't you Willie?' he said. I promised to do my best.

We were off as soon as the light was sufficiently good. Somewhere south of St Michel, Stewart signalled that an extra machine had joined our formations; this proved to be the C.O. in his 375.

The powerful machine, unencumbered by bombs, soon caught us up, flew beside us for a little while and then turned away. At the time I greatly appreciated this informal inspection, especially as both formations were complete.

As we turned north, the first rays of the sun lit up our wings and made the seven-ply shine, its light bringing fresh courage.

An hour later we were leaving the last well-known land-mark in the Grand Dutchy of Luxemburg; the air was filled with a misty radiance even at 15,000 feet, so that it was only possible to see a few miles, but I knew that I could rely on my compass.

Presently I realised that we were making excellent progress; we should have time to reach Cologne, if the pace would last. Unfortunately, one D.H.4 began to fall below and behind Bell's second raid.

'I wish he would turn back, the Huns will get him for a cert,' I thought.

A few minutes later we saw that the whole of the Rhine valley was full of fog. It struck me that this was probably only morning mist, through which the spires of Cologne Cathedral might be peeping. If we dropped our bombs immediately to the northwest of them, we should get the main station, while the E.A. would be unable to leave their aerodromes.

On we went, but we saw no sign of the much-desired spires. There was now no time to be lost if we were to bomb Duren and get back to the Line before we ran out of petrol. The machine that had been left behind now turned and flew away homewards. On reaching Duren we let fly at a handsome factory.

As we turned slowly towards the south, I watched the ten machines following us round through the barrage smoke, a splendid sight not easily forgotten. The forests were beneath us again; away to the northwest was the smoke of a large town, perhaps we should ride to Aix another day.

The sky was clear of hostile aircraft, the very roar of my engine seemed to sink until I was scarcely conscious of it, so steady was the note. Only the discovery of a new railway broke the monotony of our homeward journey.

Time was passing; we had certainly come a very long way, but it would take the gilt off the gingerbread if we lost half a dozen machines through lack of petrol. At last Arlon greeted us with its fair white roads, showing that we were on the exact course; there had been nothing to go by when over the forests.

A little later Verdun was in sight, and the A.A. fire grew heavy. Something seemed to tell me that I was crossing for the last time, and I was greatly tempted to put my nose down through the last few miles of danger; I did not do this, as it would not only have been foolish but undignified.

The long run home followed its usual course; several machines landed at Ochey, and *No. 6* herself ran out of petrol at 6,000 feet. We had plenty of height, and arrived over the aerodrome at 2,000 feet.

Fearing that other machines might interfere with my landing, I told Stewart to fire distress signals, which he did many times, with great satisfaction.

Some of the officers of 104 Squadron were looking up at us as we swished quietly in 20 feet over their heads. We made a perfect landing in the middle of the aerodrome, climbed down and walked to the office feeling very tired.

Yes, we had been to Duren, and they must have heard us in Cologne, but the Rhine Valley was full of fog.

Mackay turned back shortly before we reached Duren; he appeared to be losing height and I did not think he could have reached the Line.

Would Yates mind taking out a can of petrol to *No. 6* and bringing her in? He must take care, as the others were landing.

After a wash, some more breakfast, and a little sleep, I felt much better, and went to the office to help the new observers make out their reports.

Everyone was pleased, in a weary sort of way, the most cheering news being that Mackay had landed a mile inside the French Line at Verdun.

That evening Stewart and I were invited to dinner at Wing H.Q. As we walked down there, a great mass of dark cloud began to rise in the west. The fine weather was at an end.

A period of enforced idleness followed. Walmsley was told that he was to return to England after nearly a year with the squadron; so he handed his flight over to Bell, and careered madly around on 'N' at a height of 50 feet, with Ward smiling calmly in the back seat. The squadron was much scandalised, yet inclined to overlook this one regrettable incident in an otherwise blameless life.

A few days later Silly, who was in command of the squadron while Gray was on leave, rang me up to say that I had been given the D.F.C., and that I was to hand over my flight to Mackay, as I was going home shortly. I was not to cross the Line again.

The weather cleared, but poor Bell had no sort of luck with the raids. On his very first show as leader, he was shot in the petrol tank by a Hun, and obliged to resign his place to his deputy. Imagine the feeling of this unfortunate officer as he flew homewards, drenched to the skin by petrol, which continued to pour over him and leave a white mist behind his machine, fired at by E.A. using incendiary tracers! He was completely defenceless, as his observer could not reply for fear of setting his own machine on fire.

The raids failed to reach their objective and returned, losing a machine on the way. The show was again attempted in the afternoon, but four machines returned and the rest became scattered owing to clouds; Bill Pace, however, crossed all by himself, and bombed the railways at Metz.

That evening Silly spoke to the flying officers of the squadron, and put the situation squarely before them.

Never had the squadron had such a bad day; machines had come back through minor defects, which should have been found and remedied before starting; machines had failed to keep formation, and the show had been ruined. The fair name of the squadron was endangered.

Twelve machines were safer than seven or eight, when it came to a scrap, and they could expect a scrap every time they went over.

He was going to Frankfurt in the morning with twelve machines. Twelve machines would cross, and twelve machines would carry on until they reached their objective or were shot down; those were the orders.

The little meeting dispersed into the growing dusk filled with a sense of impending disaster; Silly was thinking of the old days, he had not counted with the D7 Fokker, it was said.

The next morning I watched them go; Silly was out on the aerodrome with the first raid, waiting for the second to get into place. Up went the light, twelve machines were taking off – how many would return?

An hour later two close formations were flying over the Northern Vosges at 15,000 feet, their way blackened by unpleasantly accurate A.A. fire, for the sky was covered by high white cloud.

Presently, however, the shelling ceased, as flight after flight of Huns raced in to the attack.

On swept the raids, the fighting became more and more intense; every British machine was shot about and as many as forty scouts were counted.

Ludwigshafen lay to the right, under its pall of smoke by the River; Kaiserslautern to the left, red brick in its circle of green; one after another these alternative objectives were left behind by the gallant twelve.

The observers were running short of ammunition, but they got a Hun in flames in the nick of time, while several others had been shot down out of control. Meanwhile Stewart had been killed.

On reaching the objective, the raids were attacked by thirty E.A., but over a ton of bombs were dropped with good results.

Having failed to stop the raids, and having suffered a number of casualties themselves, the E.A. now followed at a respectful distance. Far away in the pale sunlight lay the cities of the Rhine, a black cloud of barrage smoke over each.

Southward sailed the raids, still keeping close formation; passing once more through the heavy Archy near the Line, they returned without further opposition from the enemy.

First we heard the distant murmur of engines, then we caught sight of five machines high up in the clear morning air; then another of six. If they had been to Frankfurt and had only lost one machine, they had indeed been fortunate.

Then I saw my old machine, which Bridgland was flying, come racing in all by herself; no one could be seen in the observer's cockpit, the Lewis gun was sticking straight up in the air; I knew that Stewart was dead …

Presently the others began to land …

His, the finest show ever carried out by any squadron, shows that a determined leader can triumph in the face of what looks like certain disaster.

No. 6 was so badly shot about that she could not be rebuilt. She had had a good year with the squadron; she had done perhaps a hundred shows, she had dropped many tons of bombs, and had destroyed quite a number of E.A., besides taking countless photographs. I felt that her end was fitting.

That afternoon the Colonel came over to Azelot; a reconnaissance was to be carried out, the squadron was short of people who could do it and would I go?

'Is it important, Sir?' I asked, for I really did not feel up to the task.

'Oh no, Willie, it doesn't matter.' The Colonel went himself, much to my disgust.

The next day came, 'Baldwin's on the phone, he wants to speak to you.'

'Yes, Sir?'

'Oh is that you Willie? Colonel Bloomfield wants to go to Paris tomorrow, will you take him?'

'Yes, Sir.'

'Sure you feel up to going?'

'Oh yes, I think so Sir.'

Stewart's funeral was the next day; had I been at the squadron, I should, of course, have gone.

It may have been only a coincidence, yet I always looked upon my being sent away as a kindly action on the part of our Wing Commander, who saved me from a very painful ordeal.

The next morning was beautifully fine. Away we sailed in Gray's double-gun 375. Having called at the new Aircraft Depot, we flew to Le Bourget via Troyes.

Colonel Bloomfield gave me lunch at the Ritz. After lunch, he went over to talk to General Sir Hugh Trenchard who sat with his staff at another table, and I had the honour of being introduced to the great man.

The trip home, by way of the recent battlefield of Château Thierry, was very interesting. A slow spiral in the sunset and a quiet landing followed, the last I was to make in France. I was given a very generous send-off next day, when I left for England.

The work of the squadron went on, long shows being carried out right up to the end of the war.

APPENDIX

LETTER FROM CAPTAIN WILLIAMS TO HIS MOTHER, DATED 15 MARCH 1918

Words that are unclear are italicised.

Dear Mother

We had a nice game of football yesterday evening, going down the field after the ball one forgets the war and all its 'Ruthlichluiet' it was grand to do that for an hour! We have got such good new fellows, Bridgland, Whitelock, Keep etc. Legge plays the [*piano*] beautifully. Also some of the new observers are jolly keen, especially a little Canadian who cannot be more than 18 and [*months*] and is as keen as mustard.

Today I went out alone with Captain Ward MC as Bradley is still frozen. We went miles over Hunland but could not see the objectives for huge banks of low clouds. On the way home we saw a formation of 4 Hun scouts about our level and nearer the lines. Whether they did not see us as they were probably looking towards our lines or what, I don't know but they flew parallel with us towards their front lines for about 20 minutes and when we got to the lines I crossed and they began a line patrol as I thought. When I had begun to lose height to come home I saw our archy going away to the right, so put on the engine again and hurried towards it. After about ten minutes I saw that our 4 foes had been so foolish as to get about 3 miles our side of the lines and were flying along away from me. That was a grand moment – I thought we were nearly going to have a scrap at any rate on the lines but oh dear no, nothing doing! The four chaser pilots saw us coming on what they described the other day as 'super battleplane' (but what I should call our venerable two seater!) and did they wait? No, two who were highest above us escaped scot free back across their lines without firing a shot or even coming into range, the one nearest the lines dived for home with us after him and the fourth, did he come to his pal's assistance? No, he tried to get home by another route as quickly as possible. Just before I opened fire I looked around and saw Ward standing at his gun with a broad smile on his face. We were just too late to cut our Hun off from the lines or get into deadly range of him but I got him well in my sights and gave him a long burst of fire, I could see my tracers going all over them of course he was doing every possible trick to get out of the fire. The Hun archy put up a barrage between us and him which was pretty hot as he crossed very low (They had crossed our lines at 18,000 at first!) us knowing that it would be fatal to go on flying straight I did a climbing turn and let Ward have a shot. We then went after Hun no 4 who was just diving across the lines some way away and had a good shot at him too, but all the firing was at such long range that we could not expect to bring any one down, but I have never seen anyone with such lack of discipline and courage. They never fired a shot the whole time! Importantly being an old scout pilot they have made me deputy leader of raid no. 2 which means looking after the back of the formation on bomb raids! Just because I shot down a Hun at – the other day and drove off others whilst covering our retirement lots of the fellows think that if I am there then they are safer, whereas of course I shall not be able to do anything against this cowardly method of about 20 Huns sitting behind us at long range and ?? us! I do not intend to let the boys I am supposed to guard down though, and if things get too hot may God give me the courage to turn around and either drive them off or go down fighting for I've never turned my back upon Hun or devil yet! If the Lord is very kind I ought to get leave in quite a short time now unless leave is stopped. Everyone is very cheerful.

One thing I will say for the enemy they have some jolly stout fellows amongst them, and when it comes to burying our dead they always do it nicely and put over the graves 'Brave English Soldiers who died for their Fatherland in the fighting by Ypres July 1915' for example and what more glorious thing could be written over one's grave than '*Tapfer Englisher FLièger im Lufer Kampf gefallen*'. There are certain names of places that will always hold glorious but sad memories for us in the RFC such as Vitry-en-Artois, Donai, Cambrai, Senain, Orchie, Valoucienne, Mons, Lille, Courtrail, Goutrode Ghent etc, etc. and we are adding more to the list! I cannot say 'Vitry en Artois' without thinking of the crown of Red Devils of the splendid 'Circus of Death' fighting with our splendid little brown scouts; there were gathered the very flower of Europe in the glorious days of '17! Well I hope I have a little of the old spirit of those days left and I hope I shall still be able to find a few of the Huns as gallant foes as ever. I hear people who are asking is a cart-load of monkeys the limit! Love to the children (James and all). Splendid results the other day again. The CO has been jolly nice to me all along but I am in the [*kingdom*] of the prophet Daniel now and then!

   Your loving son
   Eric

PS There is no harm in letting people know I am getting on and that I got a second pip last August if it pleases them. I have got the mascot the little union jack braves the battle and the breeze (200 miles an hour sometimes!). Do not worry I shall not go down before anytime and if I do I hope it will be in saving some fine young fellows for England. With luck I may be the same as Dick Wigan became?? after his scrap with the arabs any day now. The funny thing is nothing I did before I came here counts now! (officially). Well God bless you all my dears! I am sure Daddy would like me to do as I intend to.

   I am not going to be at all foolhardy but I must only do my duty as a man is bound to do!

   We don't want to fight, but by jingo when we do!

Letter from Captain Williams to his mother, dated 15 March 1918

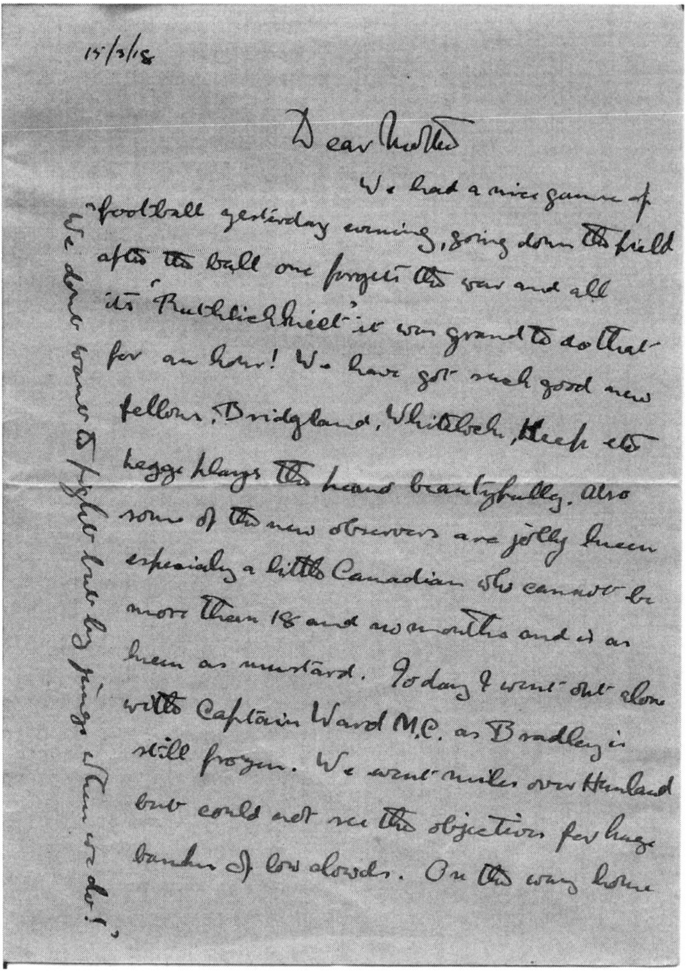

15/3/18

Dear Mother

We had a nice game of football yesterday evening, going down the field after the ball one forgets the war and all its 'Ruthlichkeit' it was grand to do that for an hour! We have got such good new fellows, Bridgland, Whitelock, Heck etc Legge plays the piano beautifully. Also some of the new observers are jolly keen especially a little Canadian who cannot be more than 18 and two months and is as keen as mustard. Today I went out alone with Captain Ward M.C. as Bradley is still frozen. We went miles over Hunland but could not see the objectives for huge banks of low clouds. On the way home

'We have to fight but by jingo when we do!'

We saw a formation of 4 Hun scouts about our level and nearer the lines. Wether they did not see us as they were probably looking towards our lines or what I dont know but they flew paralel with us towards their front lines for about 20 minutes and when we got to the lines I crossed and they began a line patrol as I thought. When I had begun to loose height to come home I saw our archy going away to the right, so put on the engine again and hurried towards it. After about ten minutes I saw that our 4 fools had been so foolish as to get about 3 miles our side of the lines and were flying along away from me. That was a grand moment – I thought we were nearly going to have a scrap at any rate on the lines but oh dear no, nothing doing! The

III four 'clever' pilots saw us coming on what they described the other day as a 'super battleplane' (but what I should call our venerable two seater!) and did they wait? No, two who were highest above us escaped scot free back across their lines without firing a shot or even coming into range, the one nearest the lines dived for home with us after him and the fourth did he come to his pals assistance? No, he tryed to get home by another route as quickly as possible. Just before I opened fire I looked round and saw Ward standing at his gun with a broad smile on his face. We were just too late to cut our Hun off from the lines or get into deadly range of him but I got him well in my sights and gave him a long burst of fire, I could see my tracers going all

IV going all over him of course he was doing every possible trick to get out of the fire. The Hun surely had up a barrage between us and him which was pretty hot as he crossed very low (they had crossed our lines at 18000 at first) or knowing that it would be fatal to go on flying straight I did a climbing turn and let Ward have a shot. We then went after Hun no. 2 who was just diving across the lines some way away and had a good shot at him too, but all the firing was at such long range that we could not expect to bring any one down, but I have never seen anyone with such lack of discipline and courage. They never fired a shot the whole time! Unfortunately, being an old scout pilot they have made me deputy leader of said No.4 which means looking after the back of the

back formation on bomb-raids! Just
because I shot down a Hun at — the other day
and drove off others whilst covering our
retirement lots of the fellows think that
if I am there they are safer, whereas of
course I shall not be able to do anything
against this cowardly method of about
20 Huns sitting behind us at long range
and peppering us! I do not intend to let
the boys I am supposed to guard down
though, and if things get too hot any day
God give me the courage to turn around
and either drive them off or go down
fighting for I've never turned my
back upon Hun or devil yet! If the
Lord is very kind I ought to get leave in
quite a short time now unless leave is
stopped. Everyone is very cheerful.

VI. One thing I will say for the enemy they have some jolly stout fellows amongst them, and when it comes to burying our dead they always do it nicely and put over the graves "Brave English Soldiers who died for their Fatherland in the fighting by Ypres July 1915" for example and what more glorious thing could be written over one's grave than "Tapfer Englischer Flieger im Luftkampf gefallen" There are certain names of places that will always hold glorious but sad memories for us in the R.F.C. such as Vitry-en-Artois, Donai, Cambrai, Semain, Archie, Valencienne, Mons, Lille, Courtrai, Gontrode, Ghent, etc., etc. and we are adding more to the list! I cannot say Vitrie en Artois without

...thinking of the crowd of Red Devils of the splendid Circus of Death nearly fighting with our splendid little brown scouts; there were gathered the very flower of Europe in the glorious days of '17! Well I hope I have a little of the old spirit of those days left and I hope I shall still be able to find a few of them as gallant foes as ever. I hear people swear as they are a cart load of monkeys an the limit! Love to the children (James and all) Splendid results the other day again. The C.O. has been jolly nice to me all along but I am in the position of the prophet Daniel now and then!

Your loving son
Eric

P.S. There is no harm in telling people how I am getting on and that I got a second pip last august. if it pleases them. I have got the medal, the little union jack braves the battle and the breeze" (200 miles an hour sometimes!) Do not worry I shall not go down before my time and if I do I hope it will be in saving some fine young fellows for England. With luck I may be the same as Dick Wigan became after his romp with the arabs any day now. The funny thing is nothing I did before I came here counts now! (officially) Well God bless you all my dears! I am more Daddy would like me to do as I intend to.

[left margin, written vertically] I am not going to be at all well for several days as a man is coming to do the only do any duty as a man is coming to do.

If you enjoyed this title from

The History Press:

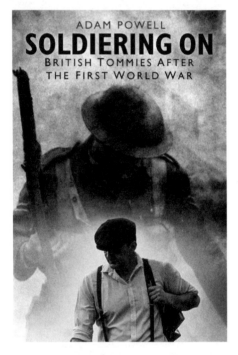

978 0 7509 9147 6

The History Press

The destination for history
www.thehistorypress.co.uk